THE RIGHT WORDS FOR ANY OCCASION

Erika Swanson Geiss

Publications International, Ltd.

Erika Swanson Geiss is an author and editor whose interests include current events, fine art, parenting, and environmentally friendly living. She is a work-at-home mom and the owner of Red Pencil Editing Services, and she *always* signs her letters with a fountain pen. This is her second book with Publications International, Ltd. Erika lives in Michigan with her husband and young son.

Louis Weber, CEO
Publications International, Ltd.
7373 North Cicero Avenue
Lincolnwood, Illinois 60712

ISBN: 978-1-4508-8361-0

Manufactured in China.

8 7 6 5 4 3 2 1

Contents

When You Need the Right Words

THE ART OF EVERYDAY WRITING seems to have gotten lost. One sign is that some college graduates do not even know how to write a basic business letter. Another sign is that some people's penmanship is simply appalling. Some have never set foot inside a stationery store, while others can't remember the last time they actually received a letter in the mail from a friend or family member.

Although there are those people who regularly write thank-you notes, few take the time to write letters for no specific reason or to personalize their thank-you notes or sympathy cards. E-mail is filled with poor grammar, awful spelling, even worse sentence structure, and sprinkled with chat-room and text-message acronyms and abbreviations. As a society, our ability to express ourselves in the written word for a variety of occasions is not what it used to be a century ago, or even a few decades ago. In many ways, the burst of new Internet technology such as instant messaging, Internet chatting, and mobile text messaging has reduced many of us to using shorthand that is inadequate for most types of written communication. This literal shorthand has diminished our collective abilities to craft a good letter with the versatility of being able to write to anyone and for any occasion.

At some point, nearly everyone will need to write a letter, memo, or e-mail. The question is, do they have the tools to write an effective one? For those who regularly write letters, are they stuck in a rut, repeatedly writing in the same way and about the same thing while changing only the recipient? What about you? Are you suddenly at a loss for words when trying to format the letter of recommendation requested by a former employee? Do you know how to tell dear Aunt Sally how sorry you are for breaking her favorite crystal bowl? Does your mind go blank when e-mailing a business acquaintance you have met only once? For these trying times (and for many others), *The Right Words for Any Occasion* will be your handy guide to writing thoughtful, tactful, personal or professional letters. It will become your tried and true writing friend.

Starting with learning how to understand letter format, voice, tone, and grammar, *The Right Words for Any Occasion* will guide you through preparing to write, from materials and formatting to the social and business correspondence you encounter on an ongoing basis. With toasts and congratulations, thank-you notes, sympathies, love letters, and even "hate mail," this invaluable book will help you put your best verbal and written foot forward in letter writing. Business issues are also addressed, from writing cover letters to handling contractors and home-related business.

Beyond social and business letters, *The Right Words for Any Occasion* also addresses academic letters, including how to write a letter of complaint to an instructor, an absence note, a request for a letter of recommendation, and so much more. Special situations are discussed, such as corresponding with people abroad as our global borders shrink and we conduct business with people around the world. This book is not designed to address every type of letter you encounter in your lifetime, but it is meant to give an overview of the letters we face in everyday life. From snail mail to e-mail, faxes and memos, this book will be your writing companion for any occasion.

CHAPTER
1
Get Ready to Write

WHEN WAS THE LAST TIME you wrote a letter? Not an e-mail, but a real, bona fide letter? When was the last time you read a *good* letter? How about a thank-you note? Are you really sure about how to write a cover letter for a new job? Do you find yourself slipping into colloquialisms when writing an e-mail, or slang and poor spelling when blogging or in an online forum? If you do write often, are you stuck in a rut, writing the same way, writing the same things repeatedly, and perhaps changing only name of the recipient? Or did someone ask you to write a letter of recommendation for them, and you were at a loss for words? Did you think your résumé described the ideal candidate for a job, but somehow you didn't get an interview? Did you unintentionally irk some colleagues, or worse, your boss, because of a quickly fired-off e-mail? These are a lot of questions to start asking yourself, and you will probably answer "yes" to at least one of them.

THE RIGHT WORDS

Writing is an art. Words can heal, but they can also hurt. Words can make or break another person's day or a business opportunity. The right words can land you that promotion or new job and countless other opportunities. The wrong words can get you nothing, or at the very least, not the results you anticipated. The written word, unlike the spoken word, is also a permanent record.

It is a delight to open, hold, and read a letter that is well written, well crafted, engaging, and eloquent—whether it is a memorandum, a quick note to a casual acquaintance, or a cover letter. Reading well-structured prose in an e-mail or blog is rewarding. You don't need to be a Pulitzer-prize winning journalist or *New York Times* best-selling author to have well-written prose and to craft your writing, no matter how ordinary the circumstance.

But before you start writing, let's make sure that you not only have the right tools, but that you know what they are and how to use them.

B.C. (Before Computers)

Before the electronic age swept us into the world of instant (or nearly instant) communications, we lived in the age B.C.—before computers. If we wanted to correspond with someone in writing, we had to sit down and compose with paper and ink or on a typewriter. The standard for writing was firmly etched—or rather, printed—upon the minds of the literate. The use of language was a skill, and rhetoric was an art. Young women and men had stationery wardrobes, and almost anyone in business knew the correct format for a business letter. Having a good pen with a nice weight, a nib that didn't stick, and fluid ink was ideal. And penmanship was nothing short of beautiful.

Today, we have the ease and simplicity that technology affords us. We can type and print letters at record speed. We can send letters and other correspondence electronically to virtually anyone anywhere, instantly, and we can communicate in real time with people several time zones away. Though we've gained in ease and simplicity, we've lost something in the process. However, with a return to some fundamental principles and a good understanding of them, you will be able to write letters and other correspondence that get noticed for all the right reasons.

YOUR WRITING TOOLBOX

According to Miss Manners in *Miss Manners' Guide to Excruciatingly Correct Behavior,* during the B.C. era, one needed a full stationery wardrobe—also known as writing paper. The stationery wardrobe consisted of small note cards, full-size 8½×11-inch sheets of paper, standard envelopes, gentleman's or lady's cards (often called visiting cards, which you would leave at the front door or parlor when visiting friends, even if the person you were visiting was at home), and sometimes one small business card with your full name on it, among other things. All of these were engraved on quality linen or rag paper and were accompanied by matching envelopes engraved with the return address.

The contemporary stationery wardrobe is not quite as elaborate. Today, you will still need to have several sizes and weights of paper and the appropriate envelopes, two good pens—one with blue ink and one with black—and if you have a computer, a printer with well-stocked black ink. It is also beneficial to have a dictionary and a thesaurus, which no home or office should be without.

Stationery Wardrobe: The Social Calling Card

To paraphrase Miss Manners, the social calling card was the equivalent of voice mail—leaving a social calling card meant that you made an attempt to make contact with a friend or acquaintance. The proper social cards are engraved and contain your title (also called the honorific), formal name, and street address. Additional information can be included if it's appropriate, such as a very short note explaining why you were visiting.

Choosing Your Materials

Paper comes in various weights, sizes, and colors—from bright white and colored copy paper to special card stock, watermarked linen, and rag paper in various shades of white, cream, beige, and gray. Each type of paper is used for different occasions and purposes—the more serious the purpose of the correspondence, the more special the paper should be. For example, you do not print a résumé on plain white copy paper or on colored paper, for that matter. Instead, print a résumé on linen paper. And for the environmentally conscious, there are versions of all of these types of paper with partial or full recycled content, so don't fret—you do not need to worry about sacrificing the environment for a good first impression. Now we'll look at each type of paper so you know what we mean, starting with the largest.

Letter Paper

Standard letter paper is 8½ inches wide and 11 inches long. It's used for longer personal letters and all forms of business correspondence—except legal writing, where you would use 8½×14-inch paper. In business, formal communications should be on bond paper and have the company's letterhead, seal, or logo on the first page. Business stationery (or letterhead) comes in reams of 500 sheets and in sets of two pages—the first page has the company's coordinates and logo or letterhead, and the second page is blank but of the same weight and quality as the first page. When paper is referred to in weight, it means the weight per 500 sheets of paper. The weight of formal business and résumé bond stationery ranges from 16 to 32 pounds—with the most popular weights in the 24- to 32-pound range. When selecting bond paper, the higher bond provides a better quality and thicker paper. Other uses for bond paper are cover letters, résumés or curriculum vitaes (CVs), business-related thank-you notes, and other miscellaneous business correspondence. For all other types of business and formal writing—including memos and reports— 20-pound, standard white paper should be used. When using bond or regular paper, the correspondence should be typed.

Notepaper

Notepaper is usually half the size of standard letter paper, roughly 8½ inches long and 5½ inches wide. It can be gum-bound or in single sheets. Like business stationery, it is often engraved or printed with the name or monogram of the individual or the business, centered on one line. If used for personal stationery, the address can also be engraved or printed on the stationery and placed at the upper right-hand corner of the sheet. Some notepaper is lined, but it does not need to be. Notepaper comes in various weights, from regular 20-pound paper to watermarked 24-pound and 32-pound linen paper or heavier card stock.

Note Cards

Note cards come in two varieties, folded and unfolded. When opened, the folded note card is the same size as notepaper. The unfolded note card is 5½ inches wide by 4¼ inches long. The folded note card can have the person's name engraved or printed on the outside if used for personal stationery, or the business seal or name in the same place if for a company. Note cards are usually of card stock—a heavy weight of paper, usually 65 pounds or more. Ideally, note cards should match the other parts of your stationery wardrobe in terms of overall color scheme and design. Both note cards and notepaper can be blank. For singular cards and their matching envelopes, make sure that yours conform to postal regulations.

Business Cards and Personal Cards

Business cards are 3¼ inches wide by 2 inches long. The name is printed on the centerline of the card with the title, company, or affiliation beneath it. The address, telephone number, and e-mail address can be at the bottom center or in the lower left- and right-hand corners. Do not confuse your business cards with a mini résumé and put more information on them than is needed. They are too small to cram a lot of extra text on them.

The great thing about business cards is that they aren't just for executives anymore. Many people, from the self-employed and freelancers to independent scholars and mothers who work from home, use business cards. Even if you aren't affiliated with a company, they can still help identify you or remind someone who you are.

Personal cards function like business cards. They were once referred to as "visiting cards" or "calling cards." Since people no longer call upon one another in person, and instead pick up the phone or shoot a text message, instant message, or e-mail, calling cards do not have the same importance that they once held. The beauty of them, however, is that when you are sending a gift or other personal communication, you can use them to add a short note or to indicate that it was you who sent the package. Because personal cards do not usually include your address, use of them assumes a certain level of familiarity with the recipient. That is, the recipient already knows your address or other relevant contact information. If you wish, however, to provide your contact information because it is nowhere else, place it in the upper right-hand corner of the card. Personal cards are slightly smaller than business cards, and there are different sizes for each gender—but that rule probably isn't as important as it once was. But, if you wish to be especially proper about your stationery, gentlemen's cards are 3¼ inches wide and 1⅝ inches long, and women's cards are 3⅛ inches wide and 2½ inches long.

Another optional part of your stationery wardrobe is a set of pre-printed invitation cards with matching reminder and reply cards and corresponding envelopes. These are a great idea if you throw a lot of formal parties. You could also have these made as you need them since there are ample printers, stationers, and engravers around.

The Old Language of Business and Social Cards

Business and social cards once had a silent language whereby folding the corners indicated short, quick messages.

Upper left: I was here, sorry not to find you in.

Upper right: Congratulations

Lower left: I'm leaving town, good-bye.

Lower right: Condolences

Envelopes

So you've got the paper, but you have to send it somehow. Just as there are several different types of paper, there are several different types of envelopes.

For standard paper, use number 9 or number 10 envelopes. Number 9 envelopes are 3⅞ inches long and 8⅞ inches wide. Number 10 envelopes are 4⅛ inches long and 9½ inches wide.

Both are considered "standard" envelopes. The envelope should also match the style of the paper—so if you are using bond paper, use bond envelopes. Letters should be folded in thirds—the bottom first, folded inward toward the printing. Using the first line of the first paragraph as your folding guide is an easy way to gauge how far to make the first fold. Bring the bottom edge of the paper upward, align, and make a crease. Next, bring the top edge of the sheet downward so that it meets the fold and crease it. If you have enclosures and are sending something very thick, either fold the pieces in half and use an envelope that is 6×9 inches, or leave the documents unfolded and use a catalog envelope that is 9×12 inches or 10×13 inches. This depends on how thick the package is that you are sending.

For memo paper, you have two options. You could use a number 6 envelope and fold the note in thirds, just as you would with a standard-size letter. Number 6 envelopes are 3⅝ inches long by 6½ inches wide. You can also fold the note in half and use an A2 envelope, which is 4¾×6½ inches.

The Ink

So you've got paper and envelopes. You're ready to write! Ah, but what to write with? That all depends on what you are writing, of course. For all writing situations, you will need a good pen. And by a good pen, I don't mean the kind of pen that you used in high school to make doodles during history class or write notes to your friends. I mean a pen with a nice barrel, a good weight—one that feels nice in your hand—and writes smoothly without skipping. In a good pen, the ink flows well and the nib (the point) is smooth but sharp. If you're writing a letter or note by hand, you will want such a pen to make the task even more pleasant. For letters that you print from the computer, you will still need to sign your name. You want your signature to look good, don't you? For letters that are printed mechanically, make sure you have enough ink. When you print the final copy of your letter and the supporting documents or enclosures, set the printer preferences on the best quality.

Now, you've got the paper, the envelopes, and the ink. But before you sit down to write, an anatomy lesson.

THE ANATOMY OF A LETTER

Like the human body, a car, or a computer, a letter has different parts to it, each of which has its own function, arrangement, and purpose. A letter is composed of ten basic parts with an optional eleventh part. The parts of a letter are:

- ❧ Heading/return address
- ❧ Date
- ❧ Addressee's name (also called the inside address)
- ❧ Addressee's address
- ❧ Salutation
- ❧ Body
- ❧ Closing
- ❧ Complementary closing
- ❧ Hand-signed signature
- ❧ Typed or printed signature
- ❧ Postscript

Letters come in several styles, but each has the same basic parts. The various letter styles are block, semi-block, and simple formats. Block and simple formats are left justified. That is, the left margin is flush—all paragraphs align with the left margin, and the first lines of paragraphs are not indented. Semi-block format is left justified except for the first line of each paragrah, which is indented. The closing and signature are placed to the right. Four spaces should be between your closing and printed name to allow space for your hand-signed signature. Letters should be single-spaced between lines and double-spaced between paragraphs.

Block Format

Below is an example of a letter in block format.

Paul Haynes
35 Winding Road
Sodona, AZ 86336

July 19, 2008

Michelle Pesci
6570 Cactus Blossom Trail
Sodona, AZ 86336

Dear Michelle,

I want to thank you and John for your generous hospitality while our house was being renovated. Alexis and I don't know where to begin with our gratitude and hope that the extended stay wasn't too much of an inconvenience. Please know that our home is always open to you, and we hope that you and the kids will be able to come to our housewarming next month.

Very sincerely yours,

Paul

Paul

Semi-Block Format

With the same letter, here is an example of semi-block format.

Paul Haynes
35 Winding Road
Sodona, AZ 86336

July 19, 2008

Michelle Pesci
6570 Cactus Blossom Trail
Sodona, AZ 86336

Dear Michelle,

    I want to thank you and John for your generous hospitality while our house was being renovated. Alexis and I don't know where to begin with our gratitude and hope that the extended stay wasn't too much of an inconvenience. Please know that our home is always open to you, and we hope that you and the kids will be able to come to our housewarming next month.

                Very sincerely yours,

                Paul

                Paul

You will notice that in the semi-block format, the paragraph is indented and the complementary closing and signature parts are placed to the right—rather than left justified, as they are in the block-letter format.

Simple Format

The simple format follows the same conventions as the block-letter format and does not contain the salutation or the formal closing parts.

G. F. Basil and Sons
2789 West Boulevard
Sodona, AZ 86336

July 19, 2008

Michelle Pesci
6570 Cactus Blossom Trail
Sodona, AZ 86336

Rate Changes Effective September 1, 2008

This letter is to inform our valued customers that as of September 1, 2008, our rates will be increasing. Transportation rates will increase by 0.6 percent and goods and services will be assessed an additional 0.4 percent tax, as stipulated by recent industry regulations.

G. F. Basil and Sons

TAKING ON THE TASK

Now that you have your tools and know your format, you can start writing. There are four steps to writing: plan, write, edit, and rewrite.

Plan Your Prose

Now that you have the tools and know-how to set up your document, you're ready to write. Always start with a draft. Some like to compose their drafts on the computer, others still prefer the B.C. method and write it longhand on paper. Either way, writing a draft gives you a chance to get your ideas out and then edit the work. Writing a draft is important because your letter is the first impression you will make, so you want it to be stellar. For short, personal correspondence, you might want to skip the draft, but it is not recommended. If the nature of the letter is serious or intense, it is wise to do a draft first so that you don't send something you might regret having in print later. Also, since you will be mailing the letter on your fine note stationery, you don't want to waste paper or have crossed out words and other edits.

Keep It Simple

In some situations, the urge is great to write long, lofty sentences worthy of Charles Dickens. But take a tip from Hemingway and write short, simple sentences. You're not writing the next Great American Novel, you're writing a letter, which means that you've got to make your point and make it quickly. Your job is to give your reader enough information and make it fluid enough so that they want to read on, and if enclosures are included, read those, too. You will occasionally need to pull out the thesaurus and use words that would make your high school English teacher proud. But use such words with caution and only when you need to make a decided impact on your reader.

Know Your Audience

Drafts allow you to tailor your letter to the person who will be reading it. In other words, you need to consider your audience. Just as you would address your best friend differently than your grandmother when in person—even though you are quite familiar with and close to both of them—the same care should be taken when writing. The same goes for writing to people in business situations or to people you don't know well.

Tone of Voice

There are six main tones of voice in letter writing: authoritative, passive, formal, casual, accusatory, and humble. Understand the various tones of voice, and don't forget to choose your tone wisely.

Authoritative: Also called the forceful tone, it is used for addressing subordinates. Using it requires being able to write in the active voice directly and clearly without being abrasive or rude.

Passive: Used when addressing superiors or people you want to please. This is an occasion where you wish to make suggestions and use qualifying terms such as "might be" or "may."

Formal: Used when addressing people that you do not know, superiors (including elder family members), or for grave situations. Proper language and grammar should be used.

Casual: Used when addressing friends and family members who are your peers and considered your equals.

Accusatory: Similar to the authoritative tone, the accusatory tone is reserved for when you reprimand or (as the name suggests) need to accuse or address the negative actions of another. When using the accusatory tone, use the active voice. Choose your words carefully so as not to sound mean.

Humble: Similar to the passive tone, the humble tone is used when making apologies, reconciliations, or offering regrets and sympathies.

Tone of Voice

Your audience establishes your tone of voice. The tone of the letter should match the formality of the letter—more serious for business issues and letters to people you don't know well, more casual for family and friends. The only exception is with business associates who are also friends. If you are writing regarding business, keep the tone professional. If you are writing about social or personal issues, avoid sending such correspondence to their office. But if you must use their business contact information, still keep the tone professional. We often blur the lines of professionalism and friendship, but you should avoid this in your writing. Your tone of voice will also help establish the vocabulary you choose, including forms of addressing the recipient. The various tones that you can use are the authoritative tone, passive tone, formal tone, casual tone, accusatory tone, and humble tone—see page 19. Each tone informs the reader of the nature of the letter and about you as the writer.

Recipients

It is always best to find out as much as possible about addressing the intended recipient of your letter. For example, if you are applying for a job, it might be a good idea to find out who the director of human resources is, even if the application states to send the application and supporting documents to the human resources department at the Big Amazing Company. This shows that you have done your homework, as opposed to showing that you are incapable of following directions. That attention to detail may be important in getting past the screening process. If you cannot get a name or any additional information, never address a letter "Dear Sirs" or "Dear Gentlemen" unless you know with absolute certainty that the people reading it are all male. Of course, assuming that all the recipients are male today is an antiquated and gender-biased point of view. Instead, opt for "To Whom It May Concern," which is an acceptable, gender-free salutation.

Writing Your Prose and Choosing Your Words

The body of a letter should have short, clear sentences written in the active voice. You are cringing, I know. Suddenly, the voice of your seventh-grade English teacher is screaming in the back of your head, and images of sentence diagrams on a chalkboard are floating in your mind. Without the active voice, sentences get wordy and cumbersome. The active voice is direct and more concise than the passive voice. There are times when the passive voice is appropriate, such as recalling a story or writing about what you've seen on your family vacation in a postcard, but as a general rule, avoid using it.

Consider your audience and the intent of your letter when deciding your choice of words and voice. Avoid long phrases and archaic and colloquial terms, especially in formal writing.

Active Voice Versus Passive Voice

Using the active voice is more powerful than using the passive voice. In short, the active voice is a sentence where the subject is doing the action. In the passive voice, the subject is acted upon by the action. For example, "The author wrote the book" is an example of the active voice. "The book was written by the author" is an example of the passive voice.

Though there are times when the passive voice may be better to use, it can lead to grammatical problems, such as awkward phrases and run-on sentences. The active voice is stronger, shorter, and more dynamic.

Length

Nobody wants to open an envelope and read a novel, which is another reason why you should use the active voice. Try to keep the overall length to one page, but no more than two. Use short, clear sentences and relatively short paragraphs. Be direct.

Not All Fonts Are Created Equal

The appearance of a letter relies on the font. Before computers and after the dawn of mechanical printing in the 15th century, fonts had to be set by a typesetter who would diligently place each letter in its appropriate spot before printing could begin. Today, there are hundreds of standard fonts, and graphic designers and other media artists develop new ones every day. Though some fonts are decorative, use a legible font if you are using a typewriter or computer. (For exceptions to this rule, see chapters two and seven.) By legible, I mean the easiest to read with respect to size, weight, and spacing. Some fonts have equal spacing between the letters. Courier is one example where each letter, no matter how wide or narrow, takes up the same amount of space. This type of spacing goes back to the typesetting days. For Courier, each plate was exactly the same dimension, and the letter was printed in the center of that plate. Other fonts, such as Times New Roman and Arial, have absolute spacing between the letters, meaning that regardless of how wide or narrow a letter is, there will always be a certain number of points between it and the next letter. You will notice that all three font examples used below (Courier, Times New Roman, and Arial) look different and take up different amounts of space even though the size of each is 12 points. Here is an example of the same sentence in each font.

`This is an example of Courier.`

This is an example of Times New Roman.

This is an example of Arial.

You can see how much more space Courier takes compared to Times New Roman and Arial because of the even spacing between letters. You will also notice that even though all three fonts are set in the same 12-point size, they do not take the same amount of space because the point size is relative to the font itself. Despite the fact that Times New Roman is a serif font, you'll notice that Arial has no serifs, and yet each letter takes up more space. (Serifs are the little "feet" on the letters, like the letters on

A Brief Explanation of Fonts

The terms "font" and "typeface" are often used interchangeably, but the term "font" dates back to the period of mechanical printing where each character was created from a cast-lead die. For the purpose of mechanical printing, a font referred to a character of a typeface that was of a single weight, width, and character spacing. Typefaces are collections of letters, numbers, and symbols that all share the same characteristics. With electronic printing and word-processing programs, the fonts are the software that describe these collections of letters, numbers, and symbols in different typefaces. Examples include Times New Roman and Arial. The variables in fonts are:

Serif and Sans Serif: Serif fonts have "hats" and "feet" whereas sans serif fonts have neither. Times New Roman is a serif font. Arial is a sans serif font.

Weight: How light or dark the print appears with respect to the thickness of the characters. Typical weights include medium, heavy, and narrow.

Width: How close the characters are placed together. Widths are normal, condensed, and expanded.

Point Size: A measure of the height of text characters in a font. One point is approximately $\frac{1}{72}$ inch, so a 72-point font means the height of your letters is one inch.

Style: How the characters "stand." Styles are Roman (standard appearance), *italic,* and **bold.**

an old typewriter.) So, why is all of this talk about fonts important? Because with formatting, the font helps create a snapshot of your letter and gives the reader all the visual clues they need when they read the letter. It is the first thing your reader sees before they actually *read* your letter.

The tradition of typesetting and printing was well steeped in understanding that a printed page needed to convey information and give the viewer a reason to read the page. Therefore, typesetters created a sense of visual clarity and organizational beauty. If text looks too dense, the print too small, and the letters and line spacing too close together, are you really going to read it? Will you just quickly skim it? If you do intend to read it, will you read it right away or will you set it aside to read later when you've got more time? You know the answer. Very few of us have time to read something that looks like it's going to be a chore to get through. This means that if you want your reader to actually read your writing and read it right away, you've got to give them a visual hook. And that visual hook is a clean, clear font that is well spaced and not too small. This is also the same reason for writing short, clear sentences and small paragraphs whenever possible.

When choosing a font, select a font with a serif and one where the letters are not spaced too close together. Avoid using the "condensed spacing" feature unless it is absolutely necessary, such as when that final word in a sentence pushes onto the next page. The best fonts to use are Times New Roman, Garamond, Book Antiqua, Palatino, and Georgia at any size between 10 point and 12 point. (The exception is when you're choosing a font for your letterhead, monogram, logo, or other text for which a stylized and creative font is acceptable and encouraged.)

Line Spacing and Margins

Most documents should be double-spaced. Letters are the exception to this rule, where the spacing between lines within a paragraph is single-spaced and spacing between paragraphs is double-spaced. With the exception of a page header, the distance from the top edge of a page to the first line of text should usually have margins no smaller than one inch in all directions. A page header, such as a business address or your name and other identifying information, should be no less than a half-inch from the top of the page, and all other margins should be set at one inch.

Mommy Cards—The New Wave of the Playground

Many moms are confronted with the question of how to exchange information with other parents when at the playground or school events. Digging through your purse or diaper bag is a pain, and writing down your information on the back of a receipt that was buried under a juice box is far from an attractive presentation. This can be especially frustrating for working mothers, who are used to presenting a business card to business associates. But you don't want to mix business with family issues, so having Billy's mom call you at work to arrange a play date isn't the best business protocol. Think of the mommy card as a mother's equivalent to the business card. Several enterprising moms and some printers now offer mommy cards. They can be as plain or as cute as you like and include your name, your child's name, and your key information. These are relatively inexpensive, and you can even design your own with a little creativity.

Edit and Rewrite—Get a Second Pair of Eyes and Ears

After you have written your draft, read it aloud. This may sound ridiculous, but reading it aloud—even to the dog—will help you hear how your writing sounds. Does the grammar make sense? Did you really convey what you meant, or is the tone going to deliver the wrong message? These are all things to consider when writing a letter, because unlike communication by telephone or in person, the reader does not have the benefit of hearing your voice or your inflection or seeing your body language—all of which are nonverbal signs and cues that we use to help determine someone's meaning. Grammatical and structural issues—for example, a misplaced or omitted comma—can create an entirely different meaning than the one you intend.

If you are reading aloud to someone other than your dog, such as someone who can actually offer good, critical, and constructive feedback, take it. (The only time this method may not be wise is sending that love letter to your sweetie.) The great thing about having your spouse, roommate, trusted colleague, advisor, or anyone you like listen to the letter is that they can let you know if the letter makes sense to someone other than yourself. It is so easy to know what you are saying and feel that what you have written is obvious, but it is another thing to communicate what you want to say in a way that someone else can understand it. Those second pairs of eyes and ears will help you realize if something sounds too harsh, doesn't make sense, has a strange flow, and a host of other potential pitfalls. Your second pair of eyes and ears will also help you catch the things that spell-check will inevitably miss—such as those dreaded typos that are, in fact, real words. You know what I'm talking about. We've all done it.

PREPARING TO SEND
YOUR CORRESPONDENCE

You have used the appropriate tools for your letter, set the margins and font accordingly, and crafted your prose to the appropriate audience. You've made at least one draft, finished the necessary edits, and are ready to send off the final piece of written work. Finally, it's time to prepare your document for mailing. If you are using the postal system, make sure your outer envelope is of the same weight and type as your paper. Be consistent with the font of your outer envelope as well. The post office does not like illegible fonts, and if the postal workers and carriers cannot read what you have written, the letter may not reach its destination in time, if at all. Before addressing your envelope, make sure you have all of the correct postal information. You should have already done that when you prepared the inside address. Most word-processing programs today provide you with the "labels" or "envelopes" function and will import the addressee's information for you to print an envelope or label. Even so, it is still good to know the parts of the envelope and how to format them— especially if the computer or printer crashes, or you find yourself woefully out of ink at precisely the wrong time. But that won't happen because you've got a stock of ink at your disposal as one of your key tools, right?

Labels Versus Printed Envelopes

For large batches of mail, such as to a group, the address label is acceptable, especially on larger envelopes. However, if your printer has the capability to print on envelopes, it is better to use this feature. Whether you handwrite or mechanically print your envelopes depends on your letter and should match the letter's style. With a few exceptions, business correspondence should always be mechanically printed.

Preparing the Envelope

Holding the envelope horizontally with the back flap facing downward, place your information in the upper left-hand corner. This area is called the corner card and should be formatted single-spaced as follows:

> Mr. Alvin Gerber
> 1234 Main Street
> St. Clair Shores, MI 48081

But if Mr. Gerber is writing from his place of business, the format is this:

> Mr. Alvin Gerber
> Suite 23
> XYZ Corporation
> 5000 Main Street
> St. Clair Shores, MI 48081

You will notice that Suite 23 appears before the name of the company. It intuitively seems incorrect, but the post office likes to see addresses in the location order of smallest to largest. The same rule goes for the addressee's information. Some people put their return address on the back flap of the envelope. This is acceptable to the post office—they will still deliver the letter—but it might become a nuisance if your postal worker, who has to flip over the envelope to figure out the return address, has a lot of undeliverable mail to sort through. Some will argue that it's best to just put the return address on the front of the envelope.

Addressee Information

The addressee's information, also called the delivery address, is placed on the center front of the envelope and should be formatted as follows:

> Ms. Beth Snyder, CEO
> Suite 100
> ABC Corporation
> 7600 Big Oil Avenue
> Houston, TX 77506

Be sure to place the address high enough on the envelope to accommodate the bar code that the post office may print on the letter after it is received. Also, make sure that the address is not so high that it interferes with cancellation or franking of the postage. According to U.S. Postal Service guidelines in *A Consumer's Guide to Mailing*, you should

- print or type your return address in the upper left-hand corner on the front of the envelope.
- use a stamp or postage meter to affix the correct amount.
- clearly print the delivery address parallel to the longest side of the package or envelope.
- not use periods or commas for international packages and letters.

The post office also suggests that the address text be printed or typed clearly so that the address is legible from an arm's length away.

Special Addressing Circumstances

International addresses should be printed in all uppercase letters and should conform to the following specifications set forth by the U.S. Postal Service:

If possible, addresses should have no more than five lines. The full address should be typed or legibly written in English—using Roman letters and Arabic numerals—and should be placed lengthwise on one side of the item. An address in a foreign language is permitted if the names of the city, province, and country are also indicated in English. Global Express Guaranteed destination addresses must be written completely in English.

The last line of the address block area must include only the complete country name (no abbreviations) written in uppercase letters.

Foreign postal codes, if used, should be placed on the line above the destination country. Some countries prefer that the postal code follow the name, while others prefer that it precede the city or town name. The following shows the order of information for the destination address, which should be single-spaced:

Line 1: NAME OF ADDRESSEE

Line 2: STREET ADDRESS OR POST OFFICE BOX NUMBER

Line 3: CITY OR TOWN NAME, OTHER PRINCIPAL SUB-DIVISION (such as PROVINCE, STATE, or COUNTY) AND POSTAL CODE (if known)

Note: In some countries, the postal code may precede the city or town name, so follow the postal conventions where the letter or package is being mailed.

Line 4: COUNTRY NAME (in uppercase letters and in English)

The following are examples of properly formatted delivery addresses for an international letter:

MS JOYCE BROWNING
2045 ROYAL ROAD
LONDON WIP 6HQ
ENGLAND

MS JOYCE BROWNING
2045 ROYAL ROAD
06570 ST PAUL
FRANCE

The following format should always be used for destination addresses to Canada:

MS HELEN SAUNDERS
1010 CLEAR STREET
OTTAWA ON K1A 0B1
CANADA

Notice that for Canadian address, the province abbreviation is placed between the city and the postal code. Also, pay attention when describing postal codes; they are only called "zip codes" in the United States. Zip is the acronym for zone improvement plan, and its use was started in the 1960s in order for the postal service to better handle increased volumes of mail. The sender's address (return address or corner card) should also be in uppercase letters, and the country written on the line below the city, state, and zip code. So, if Mr. Gerber from our previous example is sending a letter overseas, his address should look like this:

MR. ALVIN GERBER
1234 MAIN STREET
ST CLAIR SHORES, MI 48081
USA

Alternatively, you can write out UNITED STATES or UNITED STATES OF AMERICA instead of USA.

Postage

Make sure that your letter has the correct postage for domestic or international mailing. Postage rates depend on the weight and size of the letter including any enclosures. Postage is affixed or printed on the upper right-hand corner of the envelope and should not have anything over it, such as tape. You can determine the correct postage by taking the letter to the post office, or if you have a postal scale available to you, using it to calculate the correct postage. For mailed items requiring inserts and return cards, such as wedding invitations, you should consider the weight of the entire package before purchasing your stamps and mailing your documents.

Before the U.S. Post Office Was Pony Express

Pony Express was a mail delivery service that operated in 1860 and 1861. It was comprised of men who rode ponies or horses carrying letters and small packages between St. Joseph, Missouri, and Sacramento, California, a 1,966-mile trip. The Pony Express was the fastest mail service at that time, delivering a letter or package in ten days or less. Before Pony Express, a delivery traveling the same distance took more than three weeks to arrive.

The Pony Express operated at all times of day and night no matter the weather. The quickest trip between St. Joseph and Sacramento came in March 1861 and took only seven days and 17 hours. This particular run carried a copy of President Abraham Lincoln's first inaugural address.

Filling the Envelope

This section may seem like a no-brainer, but it is important because sometimes the presentation of the opened envelope is just as important as the meat of your letter. For a simple letter that is no more than two pages and contains no enclosures, fold the letter as described in the envelopes section and insert it into the envelope so that the top flap is facing down. This way, the recipient will immediately see from and to whom the letter is addressed and the first line of the letter when he or she opens it. For simple letters with enclosures that require a larger envelope, place the enclosures behind the cover letter in the order in which they are to be viewed and place them in the envelope so that the text faces the back of the envelope. This way, the recipient can immediately see who it's from and to whom it was sent without having to turn the letter over.

Cards

Cards should be placed in the envelope with the fold facing down and the front of the card facing the rear of the envelope. This is so the card is not accidentally cut if the recipient uses a letter opener with a sharp edge. It also ensures that if there are any enclosures in the envelope, such as short notes, photographs, or money, they stay near the fold of the card and also have less chance of becoming victim to the sharp letter opener.

Complex Envelopes

Wedding invitations that have multiple parts, such as reply cards and directions, are considered complex envelopes. These will be discussed more in depth in chapter two, but for the most part, reply cards should be placed inside the flap of its stamped and addressed matching envelope. The driving directions should be on top of that. Together, those are placed in the fold of the invitation, which as in the cards example, is placed in its inner envelope with the fold facing down.

The inner envelope is addressed to the recipient with the person's name only, and that is placed with the flap side up. The front of the envelope should be placed in the outer envelope, facing the rear of the addressed outer envelope. The outer envelope, of course, is addressed properly according to the previous guidelines described.

Now, off you go to mail your perfect presentation of well-written letters and beautifully arranged packages!

Tips

Do

- choose your paper according to the purpose and gravity of the letter.
- make sure that your envelopes match the paper used.
- keep a variety of stationery and writing supplies on hand.
- have a good dictionary and thesaurus handy.
- keep your letter simple, with short sentences and paragraphs.
- use the active voice in your letters.
- make sure you use complete addresses when filling out your envelopes.
- always sign your letters. If mailing a physical letter, sign it in ink above the printed signature.
- include your printed signature and contact information if sending a letter, note, or memo electronically.

Don't

- begin writing before you think about your audience. Consider the audience when choosing your tone and vocabulary before you start to write.
- have your letter be more than two pages.
- use felt-tip pens or other pens that may run or bleed.

CHAPTER
2

Correspondence for Any Situation

ORRESPONDENCE FOR ANY SITUATION COVERS the types of letters and notes encountered in both social and business writing. These include invitations for both casual and formal events, thank-you notes, letters of acceptance, letters of regret, and toasts and congratulations. Each has its own format and style, but all should be sincere, as they are the types of correspondence that can forge, solidify, mend, or renew relationships.

INVITATIONS

Invitations are one of the more common types of correspondence you'll write or receive. Dinner parties, graduation parties, birthdays, weddings, and baby showers are just a few occasions that call for invitations.

Invitations officially alert people of an event. They should include information about the event, including its day and date, time, location, a reply date, and a method for the recipient to reply.

Invitations can be either formal or casual, depending on the event you're hosting. The type of invitation should, therefore, match the formality and type of event. Invitations should be sent so that the invited have enough time to reply and make plans to attend, and the hosts or event planners can fully plan for the number of anticipated guests. With the exception of an impromptu gathering, invitation lead time is crucial—especially if you expect to have any guests attend your function. This includes your closest friends and family members who may already know about the event you have been excitedly talking about for weeks. Remember, people are busy with obligations to their own families, work, and other social, civic, or religious duties, so don't assume it's actually on their calendars just because you've been casually chatting about it for a month.

Though some view sending invitations as a pain, they also help you out—assuming the recipients of the invitation take the time to reply in a timely fashion. Which brings up another point—if you happen to receive an invitation, even if it's from someone as close to you as your next-door neighbor, best friend, or sister-in-law, you should take the time to reply in the manner requested in the invitation. You don't want to get deleted from their list of people to invite to future events. (I think even Miss Manners would agree.) If you replied stating that you would go, but some other more pressing matter will prevent you from attending, make sure to inform the host as soon as you know of the change. But remember, you accepted an invitation, so you can't just accept a better invitation. If you're not yet sure if you'll be able to attend the event because of another engagement, do not officially accept. It's a good idea to contact the host as soon as possible and let them know you're unsure about being able to attend but that you'll let them know as soon as you have more information.

For the most part, invitations should be simple. The basic anatomy of an invitation is:

Host's name
Event
Day and date
Location
Time
Reply date and method with the contact information

The specific information in an invitation and its overall style inform the recipient of the type of event and the degree of formality. In the days before telephones, multiple phone numbers, and e-mail addresses, the type and style of the invitation also indicated the type of attire to wear, so you never had to wonder what level of dress to put on for the events to which you'd been invited. As a general rule, your attire should be more formal according to how fancy and formal the invitation is and how late in the day the event is scheduled, unless the host specifies otherwise in the invitation itself. For example, a wedding will be held at 7:30 P.M. in the evening, but the invitation specifically states "costume party," "come as you are," "business casual," or "white tie," to name a few. Before standard dress became more relaxed, "formal" meant "white tie" and "informal" meant "black tie." In contemporary modes of dress, "formal" usually means "black tie." Men, that means you're expected to break out the tuxedo, and women, that means a long dress or ball gown.

You can either start with preformatted invitations or you can create your own template. For those who like the do-it-yourself method, there are many publishing and word-processing programs you can use to make your template.

For the incredibly proper who have a full, traditional stationery wardrobe as described in chapter one, this is where you use your invitation cards. If you are using a preformatted invitation, such as a boxed set of themed invitations or your personal invitation cards, legibly write the information by hand. It is better to write in cursive or script, but you can also print if your cursive looks like the directions on a physician's prescription pad. Whichever you choose, be sure the presented information is legible, clear, and that the invitation is clean. For more formal invitations, which might be printed or engraved by a professional printer, supply the text to the printing or engraving company. The formality of the event will determine the style and font of the printed or engraved invitation, unless you specifically choose a design or template from the printer's or engraver's style catalog.

How to Write It

Before you start writing your invitations, think about the event, the time, how formal the event is (black tie or casual, for example), and whether the event has a theme. Then, look at the calendar and allow enough time to address issues of food, drink, and decorations. If you are using a caterer, they will help determine when you will need a final head count. Use that date as your reply date. A good general rule of thumb is to make the reply date at least one week prior to the date of the event. Count back from your reply date (four to six weeks for informal events and six to eight weeks for formal events) to determine the target date when your invited guests should receive the invitation. In your invitation, include who is hosting the party, the day and date of the event, the time the party starts—or if it is during a set period, the time the party ends—information about the location including the address without the zip code, and a way for invited guests to reply to the invitation. Directions to the location should also be included as an insert or on a separate card or sheet of paper if it is a formal event. If there are special instructions, such as "wear something comfortable," include that information on the invitation as well.

The following examples are arranged from the least formal to the most formal.

A Casual Party

Please join Beth and Larry for their Annual Summer Beach Party!

Saturday, August 16, 2008

3:30 P.M.

3225 Beech Tree Lane

West Egg, New York

This year's theme is Tiki Party!

Hawaiian attire is encouraged.

RSVP by August 1, 2008, by calling us at 516-555-9999

Beth and Larry have sent this invitation to 50 or so of their closest friends and family, and possibly to some of their closer business associates. Ideally, the invitation has been sent out four to six weeks prior to the event, meaning the recipients *receive* the invitation four to six weeks before the event. Chances are the invited guests are local.

If the invited guests have attended Beth and Larry's annual summer beach party in previous years, they probably anticipate its occurrence and already have it on their calendars. But the invitation serves as a reminder and gives Beth and Larry enough time to adequately plan for the number of anticipated guests. Because the event starts in the afternoon and is a beach party, the recipient can assume the attire is beach casual, but Larry and Beth have also said directly in the invitation that Hawaiian attire is welcome at the event. This type of event can either be designed as a traditional fold-over card, a single flat card, or as a flyer—that is, on a full $8\frac{1}{2} \times 11$-inch sheet of paper. A flyer seems to be a more popular option today for casual parties and events.

You may have noticed that the response line does not say "Please RSVP." That is because to add "please" to the line would be redundant. RSVP is an abbreviation for the French phrase *Respondez s'il vous plaît.* To translate the phrase into English, it means "Respond, if you please." Additionally, "if you please" does not mean a response is optional. It is just a polite way of informing the invited guest that a reply is expected. One can also opt to write "Please reply by" as an alternative to RSVP. Another variant on the "Please reply" line is "Regrets only." "Regrets only" is a popular response line for invitations and means that the recipient needs to respond only if they cannot attend.

Business Casual Events

Some events are a bit more formal, and the purpose of the event is beyond a simple party. These events are often business casual or semi-formal and may be business-related. Business casual implies an event where formal wear is not required, but jeans or shorts will be entirely inappropriate and formal wear would be over the top.

The Foundation for Really Cool Stuff
announces its third annual
Founder's Day Dinner and Holiday Party
Please join us at
the Westin Hotel in the Sherman Ballroom
1 Huntington Avenue
Boston, Massachusetts
Friday, December 12, 2008,
6:30 P.M. to 11:30 P.M.
for dinner, dancing, and awards
Please reply by November 30, 2008,
by calling Julia MacMurtrie at
617-555-1234

The location—a four-star hotel—and time of day indicates that the event is business casual or semi-formal. Indicating the overall plan for the evening also informs the recipient about what to expect. As with Beth and Larry's annual summer beach party, this invitation will have been sent out so the recipients will receive it by November 1, 2008, if not earlier—especially to account for the Thanksgiving holiday. Around the holidays, it's wise to give people enough time to reply because they are often very busy.

Formal Events

Invitations to formal events, such as weddings, black-tie or white-tie events, or anniversary parties should be engraved or professionally printed on card stock or good quality bond paper. Unlike less formal invitations, these invitations include a reply card. The reply card is the response that the recipient will return to the host of the event, which we'll discuss later in this chapter.

Although the overall language of a formal invitation is the same as for other invitations, the phrasing of the opening line will vary depending on who the hosts are.

Formal Wedding Invitation from Parents

Mr. and Mrs. Jonathan Blake

and

Mr. and Dr. Anthony Edward

Request the honor of your presence at the

Marriage of

Miss Elizabeth Ann Blake and Mr. Michael Edward

on

Saturday, the seventeenth of May, two thousand and eight,

Two-thirty in the afternoon

at

Our Lady of Hope

1234 Hope Lane

Chicago, Illinois

Reception to follow at the estate of Mrs. Wilma Andrews

60972 Oxbow Road

Chicago, Illinois

In a formal invitation, all words excluding titles are written out. It should also be noted that as an alternative to the convention of writing "Mr. and Mrs." or "Mr. and Dr.," the first and last names of the parents could be written out either with or without their respective titles.

In this case, the first line would read:

Jonathan and Felicia Blake

and

Anthony and Sarah Edward

or

Mr. Jonathan and Mrs. Felicia Blake

and

Mr. Anthony and Dr. Sarah Edward

It is tempting to use the phrase "are pleased to" following the parents' names, but some believe it is entirely unnecessary. Of course they are pleased—the fact that there is a celebration implies pleasure with the union.

If the bride and groom are inviting the guests themselves, then the invitation is from them and not the respective parents of the couple. The rule of thumb for such formal invitations is that whoever is paying for the event gets to have their names on the invitations as the hosts.

Formal Wedding Invitation from the Bride and Groom

Miss Amanda Elyse Schoeninger

and

Mr. Matthew Jason Brockenstock

Request the honor of your presence at their wedding

on

Saturday, the twenty-fourth of May, two thousand and eight,

Two-thirty in the afternoon

at

Temple Beth El

3200 Grand Boulevard

Bloomfield Hills, Michigan

Kiddush and reception to follow

Formal Golden Anniversary Party

Susan and Jonathan Edwards,

Matthew Payne,

and

Sarah Payne

Request the honor of your presence at the celebration of

the Golden Anniversary of their parents,

Andrew and Miriam Payne,

on Saturday, the fourteenth of June, two thousand and eight,

at seven o'clock in the evening

at the Woodlands Country Club

59032 Country Club Lane

Gibraltar, Michigan

In this case, you can see that the children of the guests of honor are throwing their parents a golden anniversary party, and that the hosts of the party are listed in order of chronological age. Clearly, Susan is the eldest and is already married, and thus uses her married name. Since her husband and parents are on excellent terms, he is included as one of the hosts—even though he is not the biological child of the guests of honor. Alternatively, the invitation could have read "Susan Payne Edwards" even if Susan does not usually use her maiden name. Because Susan is the first person listed, even if all three children are "hosting" the party, the reply cards should be addressed to Susan and Jonathan Edwards. Additionally, even though the husband's name usually precedes the wife's, in this case Susan's name precedes his because Jonathan is not the biological child of Mr. and Mrs. Payne. Sorry, Jonathan and other dear spouses, but when he and his siblings host a party for his parents, his name will precede his wife's.

You will note that the Payne children did not indicate the type of dress or formality of the event. The invited guests, who are probably a mixture of family, friends, and their parents' peers, will know based on the type of invitation, the location, and the time of evening that the event is black-tie or formal.

The Reply Card

The reply card for a formal event is a smaller card that, like the invitation, is engraved or professionally printed. The reply card may note the reply-by date on the first line if it is not included in the main invitation. The reply-card envelope should, at the very least, include the address of the hosts in the addressee section.

It is not necessary, but it is a nice touch and easier on your invited guests to also include the appropriate postage on the reply card or on the envelope for the reply card. Also be sure that the reply cards conform to postal regulations. Other methods to reply include the letter of acceptance or letter of regret, which are discussed later in this chapter.

Reply Card

RSVP by May 1, 2008

M._____

__ *will* __ *will not*

attend the ceremony

__ *will* __ *will not*

attend the reception

The invitation and the reply card are placed in a foil-lined envelope, often with liner paper between the invitation and the reply card. Other formal or otherwise solemn events follow this same convention.

Ways to Respond to an Invitation

Always reply in the manner stated on the invitation and with the same degree of formality of the invitation.

Acceptable ways to reply are:

- ✉ Handwritten note of acceptance
- ✉ Handwritten note of regret
- ✉ Reply card (included with the invitation)
- ✉ By telephone (for informal invitations only)
- ✉ By e-mail (for informal invitations only)

Rites of Passage

Aside from weddings, there are other significant periods and rites of passage in one's life that warrant celebrating. As we go through life, the transition from childhood to adulthood is a special time marked by religious, secular, or cultural ceremonies. Sometimes these ceremonies overlap, occurring within a short number of years. Bar and Bat Mitzvahs, confirmations, cotillions, *quinceañeras*, and sweet sixteen parties are just a few. Other rites of passage can occur earlier or later in a person's life, such as First Communion or graduation.

Bar and Bat Mitzvahs, Confirmations, and Other Religious Rites of Passage

Because these religious ceremonies are cohosted by parents and the related religious institution, there are two parts to these events—first, the actual ceremony, where guests will bear witness to the spiritual and cultural transition of the candidate; and second, a small reception or party in honor of the young person who has entered a new stage in their spiritual journey. As with other events, the formality of the invitation matches that of the corresponding party. These milestones are important, but remember that the main event celebrated is the religious rite of passage and not the bash afterward.

Bar or Bat Mitzvah

Mr. and Mrs. Jacob Steinman
Request the honor of your presence as
Alexis Steinman
is called to the Torah as a Bat Mitzvah (or Bar Mitzvah)
on
Saturday, May 17, 2008,
at
Ten-thirty in the morning
at
Congregation Beth El
151 Maple Leaf Lane
Rochester, New York
Kiddush to follow

A secondary invitation may also be included to a reception, party, or gathering that is held after the main event. The beauty of using a second invitation is that you can be selective in who is invited to the nonreligious part of the event, if you so choose.

For example, if the parents' closest friends and colleagues are invited to the religious ceremony but the parents prefer they not attend the reception or party, they may only receive the primary invitation. If the parents only wish to invite the Rabbi and his wife, family members, close family friends, and a few of their child's closest friends to their home afterward, they can do so tastefully with a secondary invitation.

A secondary invitation can be used for any event with more than one part. That includes any event with a ceremony, rite, or service, such as weddings or anniversaries with a religious ceremony or renewal of vows beforehand.

Secondary Invitation

> *Please join us for a small party in honor of*
> *Alexis's Bat Mitzvah*
> *From 4:00 P.M. to 7:00 P.M.*
> *at our home*
> *5677 Baldpate Hill Road*
> *Hilton Head, South Carolina*
> *Regrets only 724-555-0981*

Both parts of the invitation should be included in the same exterior envelope. The invitation to the ceremony does not need a specific reply card, unless there are space limitations.

In the event of Confirmation or First Communion, where several candidates may be accepting the rite at the same time, the church may provide invitations or a template for invitations. These ceremonies are sometimes held in conjunction with usual Sunday services or Mass, and an announcement of the ceremonies and the names of the candidates may be published in the church bulletin or newsletter. If the church does not provide invitations beyond what is printed in the bulletin or newsletter, parents can send out their own to notify the people they would like to invite to the ceremony who are not members of their church.

Because both of these ceremonies are one of several Christian initiation rites that a person may take over the course of a lifetime (for example, both are one of the seven sacraments for Catholics), it is best to keep the invitations simple, such as on a flat card. An additional reply card is optional, but you will want to include reply information on the invitation. Other similar religious events include baptisms, taking of religious vows or Holy Orders, and confirmations into a faith for the converted—the latter of which is usually done in adulthood. The following example presents the events that both the church and the parents are hosting, rather than a separate card for each.

First Communion or Confirmation

Please join us in bearing witness as
Chandler Francis Ablemarle
makes his
First Communion
on Sunday, June 22, 2008,
at eleven in the morning
at St. John the Evangelist Church
2300 Westlake Street
Minneapolis, Minnesota
Light reception honoring the new First Communicants
to follow immediately after the ceremony in the church hall.
Luncheon to follow the small reception
at The Big Bear Lodge
5700 Westlake Street
Minneapolis, Minnesota
Please reply by June 7, 2008,
218-555-9876

Alternate text for the lines "makes his First Communion" or "makes his Confirmation," "is baptized," "is confirmed," and so on. A sweet touch for parents raising their children in the same faith and within the same physical church and who will undoubtedly be sending several of these invitations over the course of the child's lifetime is to make a themed template so that for each new sacrament or religious initiation received, they only need to change the ceremonial subject line and appropriate dates or reception venues. Don't forget to save the template to a disk or external hard drive.

Cotillions, *Quinceañeras*, Sweet Sixteen Parties, and Other Secular and Social Rites of Passage

Most people will experience both religious and secular or social rites of passage. Social and secular rites of passage include graduations from high school, college, and other institutions of higher education, cotillions or debutante balls, sweet sixteen parties, *quinceañeras*—a Latino tradition—and proms. These events represent the presentation of a completion of a stage, whether in one's education or professional life or marking a new chronological age that may also come with new responsibilities. In some ways, the cotillion and *quinceañera* are secular equivalents of the Bar/Bat Mitzvah or Confirmation, which represent a transition from childhood into adult society.

Invitations to graduations are usually provided by the school through the graduation committee or Dean's office. Oftentimes graduates are given a set number of invitations—sometimes they're issued tickets depending on the size of the school—and they don't need do anything further. If the parents of the graduates or the graduates themselves plan to host an event after the ceremonies, they should send out separate invitations.

The separate invitation, or secondary invitation, should only be for the party and not include the graduation, since capacity for the graduation ceremonies is predetermined. Don't worry about offending people who want to attend the graduation ceremony—they will understand the space limitations and will be honored that you wish to celebrate with them, even if they don't get to attend the actual ceremony and physically see the graduate receive his or her diploma.

Cotillions, *quinceañeras*, proms, and other social rites of passage are often formal affairs, requiring a lot of advanced planning and are steeped in social and cultural tradition. It is recommended that invitations for these events be sent out six to eight weeks in advance, especially if a formal dinner will be included.

Graduation Party

Mr. and Mrs. Andrew Forman
Invite you to a barbecue to celebrate the scholastic achievement
of their son Robert,
who recently graduated from William J. Clinton High School,
on Saturday, June 7, 2008,
at 4 P.M.
at 58 Holland Road
Wilkes-Barre, Pennsylvania
Kindly reply by June 2,
570-555-9162

Cotillion or *Quinceañera* (Hosted by the Parents)

Mr. and Mrs. Ronald Robins
Invite you to a small private dinner-dance
in honor of their daughter
Graciella Elyse
on Saturday, the fifth of April, 2008,
at
seven in the evening
at
The Oak House
9872 Appleton Street
St. Petersburg, Florida
The favor of a reply is requested by March 19, 2008.

The reply cards for each of these events would follow the same formula as discussed earlier in the chapter. If the cotillion or *quinceañera* is being sponsored by a group or organization, and several girls will be making their social debut at the same function, the invitation could alternately read "the annual debutante ball" instead of naming the debutante specifically.

Note that when sending invitations to unmarried people, etiquette dictates that only the people named on the invitation are actually invited. If the unmarried people are engaged or are in an otherwise long-term relationship, both names should be included on the invitation.

"And Guest"

If the invitation does not include "and guest," do not contact the host or hostess to ask if you may bring a guest. If they wanted you to invite you with a guest, they would have taken the time to find out the name of the person you would be bringing.

If the host or hostess does include "and guest," include the name of the guest on your reply card. If you are invited with a guest, however, it does not require that you bring one.

Children's Parties

Invitations to birthday and other parties for young children that fall outside the realm of rites of passage can have a theme that matches the party theme, but they should be simple.

When preparing and sending your invitation, even for the youngest of socialites, it is important to be aware of the lead time. Chances are your children and their friends are being invited to the same parties and events, and that every family—just like yours—has multiple obligations and social commitments.

Child's Party

Please join Sara-Beth
for cake and ice cream
at her
Fifth Birthday Party
at 2 P.M.
on
Saturday, November 1, 2008,
at the Freys'
1249 Morning Glory Lane
Brookline, Massachusetts
RSVP 617-555-0119

Child's Party Alternative

Jason's turning seven!
Join us for cake and ice cream
at 3:30 P.M.
on
Saturday, November 8, 2008,
at the Johnson's
1249 Morning Glory Lane
Brookline, Massachusetts
RSVP 617-555-5540

———————— USEFUL WORDS AND PHRASES ————————

We invite you to share our joy.

Please join us in celebrating ___.

We request the pleasure of
your company.

We request the honor of your presence.

Join us for the happy occasion of ___.

We cordially invite you to ___.

Reception to follow.

We proudly announce ___.

___ is called to the Torah.

Join us in bearing witness to ___.

. . . as Jonathan makes his First Communion
[or is baptized, confirmed].

You are cordially invited to attend ___.

The favor of a reply is requested by [date].

Please reply by [date].

Regrets only

We invite you to celebrate the scholastic
achievement of [graduate's name].

━

You know those memories that make
you laugh out loud?
We hope you can join us to make
many new ones for ___!

━

Hoping this wonderful day is
shared with you.

━

The importance of birthdays is not
how many you've had
but rather how well you've celebrated.
Join us to celebrate well!

━

Another birthday, another year of
memories. Let's celebrate!

━

We're tying the knot!

━

Here comes the bride...

━

Here's to romance and to love.
Here's to a match made up above.

━

Three cheers for the happy couple!

━

Love and laughter. For today. Forever.
We look forward to sharing the love and laughter
with you on this special day.

━

Health. Wealth. Happiness.
Come share our joy.

─────── USEFUL WORDS AND PHRASES (continued) ───────

Two hands, two hearts, two souls. . . one love.

The sound of wedding bells rings
all the way to heaven.

It's a boy [or girl]!

Join us to celebrate our brand-
new reason to smile!

God has touched our lives with love.

Tips ───────────────────────────

Do

- ✉ use the active voice.

- ✉ keep the invitations as simple as possible, but make sure the invitation matches the formality of the event.

- ✉ mail invitations in time for people to receive them and reply to you—four to six weeks for informal events; six to eight weeks for formal events.

- ✉ include information about the event—location, time, attire (if necessary).

- ✉ be specific about special circumstances, such as "wear something comfortable," or "adults only."

- ✉ include directions to the event location.

- ✉ include a way for people to respond to the information and the date to reply by, whether with a reply card or by including your telephone number or e-mail address.

- ✉ include information about nearby accommodations when sending invitations to out-of-town guests (unless the guests are staying in your home).

- ✉ make sure names and addresses are spelled correctly.

- ✉ include the appropriate postage on reply-card envelopes.

- ✉ reply in the manner and by the date requested.

- ✉ inform the host as soon as you know of the change in circumstance if you cannot attend after stating that you could.

- ✉ write legibly when using preformatted invitations.

- ✉ have invitations to formal events professionally printed or engraved on quality paper or card stock.

- ✉ include directions to all parts of the event if the event takes place in more than one location, such as for a wedding, Bar/Bat Mitzvahs, or Confirmations.

- ✉ make sure your invitations, including small reply cards, conform to postal regulations.

- ✉ have invitations weighed at the post office to ensure proper postage before you send them.

- ✉ write dates in words for formal events: April second, and the second of April, are both acceptable.

- ✉ list names in order of seniority when there are multiple hosts. If it is at the home of one of the cohosts, that person's name goes first.

Don't

- ✉ refer to invitations as "invites."

- ✉ write "Please RSVP."

- ✉ write out the numerals for addresses in words.

- ✉ write out the titles Mr., Ms., Mrs., or Dr. in words.

Tips (continued) ─────────────────────────────

⊠ send reply cards for the religious ceremony for a rite of passage.

⊠ write Mr. Alan Evers and Mrs. Alan Evers when addressing a married couple. Instead, write Mr. Alan Evers and Mrs. Jeanine Evers, or Mr. and Mrs. Evers. (Mrs. Alan Evers means she is a widow.)

⊠ address invitations to Mr. Alan Evers and Guest. There is no "and guest" in invitations.

⊠ write "are pleased to announce" on wedding and similar invitations. The event already implies that the hosts are pleased.

⊠ request extra invitations to graduations, as the size of the institution or the location of the graduation ceremony and number of candidates precludes the number of invitations that each candidate receives.

⊠ use a ballpoint or felt-tip pen or a permanent marker when writing or filling out invitations. They may skip, smudge, or bleed through the invitation.

THANK-YOU NOTES

The thank-you note is a simple yet complex piece of writing. They are simple because they are easy to find—from neat little boxed packages you can purchase almost anywhere in a variety of styles for nearly any occasion to singular cards. They are complex because they are deeply personal—both for the sender and the receiver.

Most people were raised with the notion that sending a thank-you note is the correct and polite thing to do. In fact, some are irked when they do not receive one themselves. However, some of us believe it's a waste of time and paper. For those who think of the thank-you note as some antiquated notion, many will tell you that you are sadly mistaken.

The thank-you note serves three purposes. First, it acknowledges receipt of and appreciation for what has been done, even if you verbally told the person or they were actually there when you received the gift, service, time, or whatever you are thanking them for. Second, it tells the giver something about you and your character. Thirdly, while we are all pressed for time these days, it also shows the recipient that you think well of them enough to take a few moments to write them a quick note. What a way to brighten someone's day!

The realm of thank-you notes covers those for gifts and other niceties bestowed on us as well as in the business realm where one expresses gratitude for another's time or actions. As generic as the boxed notes can be, the contents of a thank-you note should not be generic and should be written in a way that addresses the individual you are thanking and what you are thanking them for. With rare exception, should you *only* write "thank you for the gift," "thank you for your time," or if you are using a preprinted thank-you note, leave it blank aside from your signature. You should always personalize a thank-you note, which will be covered later in the chapter.

In general, a thank-you note does not need to be fancy. You don't want to write one on a cocktail napkin, but you also don't need to break the bank on fancy thank-you-note stationery. A full stationery wardrobe is very useful, but writing a simple note on clean, quality stock paper that truly expresses one's gratitude is far better than a preprinted, engraved, or embossed "Thank you" on beautifully woven linen stock if you don't include a handwritten note. And with few exceptions, don't even think about sending an e-mail or text message.

How to Write It

Think about what you want to say, write in a warm, friendly style, and use the active voice. Format the note with your name and address, followed by the date, and the recipient's name and address, using semi-block format. Personal thank-you notes can be handwritten or typed. For business-related thank-you notes, block format is acceptable and should be typed. Thank-you notes should always be signed.

General Thank-You Note

The general thank-you note is for gifts, parties, and other social events. It is usually a 4¼×5½ folded note card on good card stock. The outside usually says, "Thank You" or "Thanks," alerting the recipient of the contents. The inside is where you craft your simple, handwritten prose, and don't be afraid to add a personal touch to each one.

General Thank-You Note

Dear Aunt Susan,

Thank you for the slow-cooker and Grandma's stew recipes as a housewarming gift. You remembered how much I loved her stews growing up, and knowing how much work she put into them, you've given me an easy way to make them! When you come into town next, we'll have to sit down and chat over some warm bowls of stew. Hopefully, I can do justice to Grandma's recipes!

With much love and appreciation,

Lizzy

It should be noted that Lizzy's signature should be an actual signature. This thank-you note doesn't just tell Aunt Susan "thanks," but expresses something personal about the gift and why it is appreciated.

Whether or not Lizzy ends up using the slow-cooker except for when Aunt Susan comes into town is irrelevant—the note will make Susan feel as though her gift is truly appreciated. It also reminds Susan what the gift was for. This is important. It doesn't suggest that Susan is feeble and can't remember why she sent the gift, but let's face it, in the course of a given year, we may receive or send many gifts to a single person for birthdays, anniversaries, Christmas or Hanukkah, housewarming parties, and wedding and baby showers. The list goes on. So indicating which gift and for what is a good idea, especially if the thank-you note does not follow immediately after receipt of the gift.

Timing of a Thank-You Note

The window for sending a thank-you note varies from situation to situation, and the opinions about when a thank-you note should be sent varies as well. Ideally, thank-you notes should be sent out as soon as possible after a gift has been received. The clear exceptions for this are thank-you notes for wedding gifts, where the new bride and groom customarily have up to three months from the wedding date to respond to gifts received at or after the wedding. The reasons for such a long lead time between receiving the gifts and sending the thank-you notes in this situation is purely about the realities of time. Since the newly married couple usually goes on some sort of honeymoon after the ceremony, they return home to gifts that may have been opened prior to their leaving as well as any gifts that may have arrived during their absence— gift-givers have a year to send gifts to the new couple.

Faced with the duties of setting up their home and establishing their new life together, anyone who has been through this ritual of life knows that sitting down to write 200 thank-you notes at once would require another vacation in itself. So brides and grooms are given a bit of a break when it comes to wedding gifts. Gifts for bridal showers and bachelor parties are a different story, however. Thank-you notes should be sent within a week of the bridal shower or bachelor party. They should not only be sent to guests who brought gifts, but also to the hosts of the parties.

Unfortunately, new mothers do not get the same break as newly married couples. Thank-you notes for baby showers should also be sent within a week of the shower. For gifts received after the baby is born, even as the new mother is faced with learning a whole slew of new information, some write the thank-you note immediately upon receipt of a gift. We all know that doing so is not always possible, so a good rule of thumb to follow is to get the thank-you note out within a week of having received a gift.

Thanking a Group

Sometimes gifts are given from a group of people. The proper way to thank a group is to send a personal thank-you note to each person in the group. However, this is not always possible because you may not know which people in the group participated, such as giving a gift or donating money to a cause. In this case, it's a good idea to send the note to the group president or leader.

Thank-You Note to a Group

Dear Jennifer,

I received the gift from the ladies of the Auxiliary Club that you sent with my husband after the last Council meeting. I was so surprised when he came home with that adorable package! Thank you so much for the receiving blankets, onesies, bath toys and towels, stuffed teddy bear, and outfits. We were so touched! Please also extend my sincerest thanks and appreciation to everyone for thinking of us. I'm looking forward to attending meetings again after the baby is born.

Fondly,

Debbie

Jennifer will understand the note was intended for the women who actually participated and read the note aloud at the next meeting. Debbie fulfilled her thank-you-note duties without embarrassing the people who didn't participate in the gift giving.

Thank-You Notes from Babies and Very Young Children

Though you may be tempted to write thank-you notes in the voice of your baby or young child, it should not be done. It may seem ridiculous that your baby or young child—who is neither reading nor writing yet—has crafted thank-you-note prose. Instead, the parents should write the note in his or her own voice, expressing thanks for the gift on behalf of the child.

If you absolutely cannot override the cute impulse to pen the thank-you notes in the child's voice, save those for your closest family members, such as Grandma or a dear uncle, who may be the only people receiving the thank-you notes who will share your sense of cuteness. If the child is old enough, however, he or she can sign their name or draw a little picture as a signature. For children who are verbal but cannot write well yet, they can dictate their thanks as parents write the note, and the child can still "sign" the thank-you note.

Thank-You Note from a Child

Dear Mike and Kathy,

Thank you for coming to Matthew's first birthday party. Dan and I were so glad to see you, and we really appreciate the great train set! Matthew is quite fascinated by the engine and loves saying "choo, choo" when he plays with it. I secretly think that Dan loves playing with it as much as Matthew does. Looking forward to seeing everyone at Thanksgiving!

Love always,

Marcia

Thank-You Notes for Hospitality

Hospitality is an occasion in which people often forget to send a thank-you note. Sometimes when you're invited to an elaborate celebration or are hosted by a friend or family member for an extended stay, you don't realize just how much effort was put in by your host or hostess. Not all situations require a thank-you note, but a good rule of thumb is that it is polite to send a thank-you note for hospitality for an extenstive stay or a more involved gathering. Examples of when to send a hospitality-related thank-you note is when you stay overnight or longer at a friend's house, if someone takes care of your hotel accommodations for an event, or for being invited to an elaborate gathering. Although some may believe that the quick phone call or e-mail suffices for these situations, they do not.

Thank-You Note from Overnight Guests

Dear Marcia,

We had such a lovely weekend at the beach house, and we appreciate you and Dan hosting us. Caitlin had a blast playing "big sister" to Matthew as she calls it. Everything now is about "Baby Matthew." And there was nothing quite like watching our husbands transform into the summertime superheroes Grill Man and Burger Meister. Looking forward to having you stay with us when you come into town next month for the festival!

Much love,

Kathy

Thank-You Note from a Party Guest

Dear Brian and Liz,

As always, you threw a fabulous New Year's Eve party! I think you may have outdone yourselves this year. Thanks for inviting Michael and me to what proved to be yet another memorable evening! Best wishes for a happy new year.

Yours,

Sarah

You might have noticed something in the above examples. The letters are all from an individual even though it is implied that the thanks expressed are from the couple. This is perfectly acceptable, as only the actual writer of the thank-you note needs to sign it.

A Word on Some Thank-You-Note Customs

A recent trend during social gatherings, such as showers, is to have each of the guests fill out their address on an envelope the bride or mother-to-be supplies. This seems like a good idea on the surface, as it gives the guest of honor one less thing to do when she writes her notes. But what it does is puts the guests on the spot. What if one of them has yet to supply a gift? What will she write the thank-you note for? Furthermore, the guest of honor probably already has everyone's addresses, as in the case of a wedding, when it is highly likely that the guests at her shower are also invited to the wedding. In events such as a baby shower, where the guests are probably not going to be part of the culminating happy event, the hostess or hostesses can give the guest of honor everyone's address separately.

One very good idea during such an event—or other party where large quantities of gifts will be opened—is to have someone keep a gift log. As gifts are opened and cards are read, someone records who gave what gift. This way the honoree can aptly address his or her thank-you notes to the correct person for the correct gift.

Thank-You Notes for Monetary Gifts

Notes about monetary gifts can be somewhat touchy. Some people do not like to discuss money in any capacity, and thus writing a note that says "Thank you for the gift of $100" does not sit well.

This is the instance where you can be a bit more vague in the body of the note. Presumably, the person you are thanking is aware of how much they gave you. But you should still express the same kind of gratitude and sincerity for the monetary gift as you would any other gift.

Thank-You Note for a Monetary Gift

Dear Uncle Jonathan,

I am sorry you couldn't join us for my graduation party, and I missed you terribly. Thank you for the monetary gift you sent. I really appreciate it, and it will definitely come in handy when I start college in the fall. I hope to see you soon!

Your favorite nephew,

Nicholas

Thank-You Notes in Business

The business thank-you note is different from the social thank-you note. It should be printed on company letterhead or personal business stationery and should follow a similar format as the social thank-you note. However, there should be a higher degree of formality in the tone.

The Job Interview Thank-You Note

Many business professionals will tell you that few job candidates send thank-you notes to their recruiters, headhunters, or interviewers. This statistic is appalling, and given the low proportion of thank-you notes written, the professional graciousness and courtesy you show by sending a thank-you note will set you apart from countless other candidates for the position.

How to Write It

For a job interview or other preemployment thank you, your letter should be on the same stationery as your initial cover letter and résumé. The letter should be in business-letter format. As with all formal business letters, address the recipient with Mr., Mrs., or Ms. In the body of the letter, thank the person you met with for their time and highlight key points from the interview. The letter should be no longer than one page.

When to Say "Thank You" in Business

Thank-you notes in business are a nice touch, especially when they give you an advantage over the competition! Some business occasions when a thank-you note is appropriate are:

- ⤷ After a job interview
- ⤷ After a colleague has done you a favor
- ⤷ After a colleague has been instrumental in setting up or running an event or program
- ⤷ Upon receiving a gift or contribution

Job Interview Thank-You Note

John Smith
123 Main Street
New York, NY 10013

September 4, 2008

Ms. Melissa Bear, CEO
Bear and Company
789 West 57th Street
New York, NY 10001

Dear Ms. Bear,

It was a pleasure meeting with you today. Thank you for taking the time out of your schedule to discuss the Account Executive position and introducing me to the other members of your staff. I am inspired by the innovative approaches to customer service and customer retention that have made Bear and Company a leader in the field. I am confident that my experience, skill set, and ability to learn quickly in a fast-paced environment will make me an asset to the team.

I look forward to hearing from you about the position. If you have further questions for me or need additional information, I can be reached at 212-555-1234 or via e-mail at jsmith@professional.com.

Sincerely yours,

John Smith
John Smith

John's thank-you note to Ms. Bear informs her not only of his gratitude but makes specific reference to his interview. Surely, Ms. Bear is interviewing other candidates for the position, so his note serves to remind her who he was and why she wanted to interview him in the first place. It also shows Ms. Bear that John knows how to write a business letter and that this kind of respect is one he would probably afford other people he would work with if he were to get the position.

The Colleague-to-Colleague Thank-You Note

Thank-you notes to colleagues for a job well done or help on a project can be less formal than other business thank-you notes, but they should still sound professional. This is important even if you are writing a close colleague or someone you work with on a daily basis. They should still adhere to standard business format as well.

How to Write It

There are different ways you can choose from to write thank-you notes to colleagues. If several people were involved, you can opt to send a singular, general letter depending on how many people were instrumental. If only a few people were involved, a separate thank-you note should be written to each person with a brief detail about what you are thanking them for. Whenever possible, send a carbon copy (CC) of the same note to the individual's immediate supervisor so that the commendation can be placed in their employee file.

Unless you are writing your thank-you note for something outside the realm of business, your letter should be on company letterhead and addressed to the person's business address. Again, even if the recipient is a close colleague and friend, your letter should be in business-letter format and written in a professional tone if you are thanking them for something relating to work.

To an Individual

Company Letterhead

(Note, when using the company letterhead, there is no need to include the company address again.)

September 10, 2008

Avril Johnson
Assistant Manager
Research Department

Dear Avril,

Thank you for examining the client records that I provided regarding Mr. Smith's account. I appreciate how quickly you returned the information to me so that we could resolve his questions. I look forward to working with you again in the future.

Sincerely yours,

Michael Hooper

Michael Hooper
Account Executive
Client Services

cc: Beth Johnson, Research Department Supervisor

To a Group

Company Letterhead

September 17, 2008

Dear Fundraising Events Team:

Thank you for all of your efforts in putting on a spectacular fund-raiser! The Shooting for the Stars evening on September 13 was a success. The event generated $100,000, ten percent over our goal. Special thanks go out to Andrea Anderson, who coordinated the evening, and Charles Steinberg, her cochair for planning the event. We are looking forward to next year's event, which I am sure will be just as much of a success.

Sincerely,

Fred McCloud

Fred McCloud
Department of Leadership and Development

cc: Andrea Anderson
    William Colby
    Rachel Emerson
    Susan Murphy
    Fred Murray
    Nick Smith
    Bethany Smithson
    Charles Steinberg

Thank-You Notes for Receiving a Gift or Contribution

Thank you notes in recognition of a gift or contribution for a business entity should be short and to the point. In this case, the thank-you note serves two purposes. First, it acknowledges receipt and gratitude. Second, if applicable, it can serve as a receipt for the donor. As with any business correspondence, the thank-you note should be printed on company letterhead.

Thank-You Note for a Gift or Contribution

Company Letterhead

September 24, 2008

Dear Mrs. Contributor:

Thank you for your generous contribution of $1,500 to the Shooting for the Stars fundraiser. We are sorry you were unable to attend the event, but we appreciate your continued support of our development endeavors. We hope we will see you at next year's event, and as always, we wish you the best.

Sincerely yours,

Ross Couch

Ross Couch
Senior Development Officer
Department of Leadership and Development

Oops! Remedying the Forgotten Thank-You Note

In today's world, we are all very busy. Most of us do not have the luxury of having a staff, nor as in earlier eras, is it the sole job of women to handle the responsibilities of home and event planning. Sometimes in our fast-paced and often hectic lives, we slip and forget to write a thank-you note. Or we manage to write one but forget to mail it. Don't fret, you can still send it. A late thank-you note is better than none at all. In your belated note, be honest without sounding as if you are making excuses. Indicate to the recipient how much you appreciated the act of kindness, as well as a sincere apology for not getting the thank-you note out sooner.

Belated Thank-You Note

Dear Uncle Jeff,

We are so sorry for getting this thank-you note for the lovely doll that you sent Becca for her birthday out to you so late. I came down with the flu after nursing the kids back to health, and in trying to catch up with work and the household, I completely forgot to mail our thank-you note to you.

Becca loves the Suzi doll you sent her and has slept with her every night since Suzi arrived! I have enclosed a picture of the two of them together for you, as well as a couple of shots from the party. We wish you could have made it to the party and seen how wide her eyes were when she looked in the box. We hope you are doing well and look forward to seeing you soon.

Love,

Beth

Beth's letter was sincere and candid. Hopefully, Uncle Jeff will understand the situation, but at the very least, he won't think that Beth—on behalf of her daughter, Becca—is ungrateful.

——————— **USEFUL WORDS AND PHRASES** ———————

Friends like you are a rare treasure.
Thank you for all you've done.

May life bring you a reflection of the kindness
you've shown to others. Thank you for
your thoughtfulness.

Thanks for all you've done for me.
Next time, it's my turn.

Just saying thank you because you've been
thoughtful so often!

May you be blessed for the
kindness you've shown me.

A kind deed is like water for a flower:
It makes the heart bloom. Thanks for
planting a garden in my heart.

My "thank you" seems so small compared to
all you've done,
but it comes from my heart.

Your kind gesture will last a lifetime.

I was praying for a miracle,
and then you came along.

One person. One deed. A million thanks.

You are a gift to my life.
Thanks for everything.

Knowing you're there to cheer me on is making
things so much easier. Thank you!

Only you could have known exactly what
would make my day. Thank you for knowing
me better than I know myself.

For one person, you do an awful lot of good.

It's a comfort to know we can count on each
other through whatever life brings.

How did a person like me get lucky enough
to have a friend like you?

A good deed is a reflection of a person's soul.

Thanks for helping me make molehills
out of my mountains. What would I do without you?

You always brighten my day. I'm so grateful.

Your giving nature and unselfish ways are a
blessing to everyone who knows you.

Some people give hugs. Some people give help.
You give your all.

Your kindness touched my heart.

The way you come to the aid of others is fabulous.
You are a treasure.

Generosity is a sign of a great soul.
You're surely one.

──────── **USEFUL WORDS AND PHRASES** (continued) ────────

Kind deeds change lives. Thank you.

Sometimes simple words say it best.
Thank you from the bottom of my heart.

Thank you—for what you did, what
you said, and who you are.

You have a "gift for giving"!

I'm overwhelmed by your generosity.
Thank you so much!

May your thoughtfulness
find its way back to you.

I'm better because you're the best. Thank you.

You've restored my faith.
I'll be forever grateful.

There are no words to express my
gratitude for all you've done.

I'll always remember your kindness.
Thank you so much.

A person like you brightens the
world for the rest of us. Thank you so much!

I will always be grateful to you for
your thoughtfulness and considersation.

Tips

Do

- ✉ keep it simple.
- ✉ be sincere and gracious.
- ✉ use the active voice.
- ✉ send thank-you notes as soon as possible, if not within a week of receiving a gift.
- ✉ be specific about what you are thanking the person for.
- ✉ handwrite personal thank-you notes.
- ✉ double-check the spelling of names and titles with a reliable source, such as a secretary or administrative assistant, for business-related thank-you notes.
- ✉ use appropriate business stationery or letterhead.
- ✉ use the semi-block format for personal thank-you notes and block or memo format for business-related thank-you notes.
- ✉ sign your thank-you notes using a pen with quality ink.
- ✉ find something gracious to say, even if you aren't entirely thrilled about the gift or experience.

Don't

- ✉ use a ballpoint or felt-tip pen or a permanent marker when writing or filling out thank-you notes. They may skip, smudge, or bleed through the note.
- ✉ sign another person's name. Only the writer needs to sign the note, even when writing on behalf of another party. (The only exception is in business, where a secretary or administrative assistant may be the actual writer.)
- ✉ send personal thank-you notes to a person's business address.
- ✉ go on and on about why a late thank-you note is late. Be honest and brief.

LETTERS OF ACCEPTANCE

Letters of acceptance can be used for social and business occasions. For social events, they should be used when a formal reply is required but reply cards are not included in the invitation. For a social occasion, use your card or note stationery to write a simple note to the hosts. The note should match the same level of formality as the event.

For business events, they should be used to confirm or accept arrangements in writing. In business situations, e-mails and memos are both appropriate because of the speed and timing with which business decisions are made. However, even if you are sending a letter of acceptance in a memo or e-mail, you should use business format.

If you are sending the letter of acceptance in the mail, use business stationery and type and print the letter on your computer. This will always give your letter a professional and formal tone. In all letters of acceptance, you want to reiterate the details of the event or scenario to which you are responding.

How to Write It

For business situations, use letterhead or quality bond paper and type the letter of acceptance. In certain cases, using e-mail is also appropriate, but it should still follow the format of a written letter. For social situations, you can use your personal stationery and either handwrite or type the letter of acceptance. Letters of acceptance should match the formality of the invitation or arrangements.

Format the letter with your address (unless using letterhead), the date, and the recipient's address. Use the active voice, be brief and sincere, and don't write more than one page. Thank the reader for the invitation and be specific about the details for which you are accepting the invitation or arrangements. Tell the reader that you are looking forward to the event or whatever it is you are accepting. End with a complementary closing, followed by your name and signature.

Handwritten Letter of Acceptance for a Social Event

Dear Mr. and Mrs. Robins,

Thank you for the kind invitation to your dinner and dance for Graciella Elyse on Saturday, April 5. Roberto and I are happy to attend and are looking forward to watching little Graciella make her debut.

Very sincerely yours,

Alicia Sullivan

Business-related Letter of Acceptance

Dear Anthony:

Thank you for inviting me to speak at the "Moving Forward" symposium in February. I want to confirm that the symposium is scheduled for Wednesday, February 13, through Friday, February 15, 2008, at the Hyatt Regency. My presentation on building a business identity will be approximately 30 minutes long, with additional time for a question-and-answer period with the audience. I look forward to receiving more details from you about the event particulars. Please let me know which type of audio-visual and multimedia equipment will be available.

I am looking forward to hearing from you and to working with you once again.

Yours sincerely,

Jules Madison

Jules Madison
Madison Associates

LETTERS OF REGRET

Similar to letters of acceptance, letters of regret can be used for both social and business situations. They are a polite way of informing the recipient you are unable to attend an event or cannot make the commitment to the offer in an invitation.

Letters of regret can also be used to counter an earlier acceptance of an invitation or commitment if a more pressing matter precludes your attendance. If this is the case, you should inform the person you're writing to as soon as you know you cannot attend or participate.

In business situations, you may be invited to not only attend an event, conference, or class, but also to speak or in some way participate. For this type of situation, it is especially important to let your host or hostess know you are unable to make the commitment so they have adequate time to find someone else to take your place. No matter the situation, it is always wise and polite to send a letter of regret if the invitation calls for one.

How to Write It

As with letters of acceptance, follow the same guidelines for letters of regret. For business situations, use letterhead or quality bond paper and type the letter of acceptance. In certain cases, using e-mail is also appropriate, but it should still follow the format of a written letter. For social situations, use your personal stationery and handwrite or type the letter in semi-block format.

Letters of regret in response to an invitation should match the formality of the invitation or arrangements. Format the letter in block format if it is business-related or semi-block format if it's personal. Include your address (unless you're using letterhead), the date, and the recipient's address. Use the active voice, be brief and sincere, and don't write more than one page. Start by thanking the reader for the invitation and state that you wish you could attend or participate. It is not required to give a specific reason why you cannot attend, but you can if you would like by including a brief explanation.

Social Letter of Regret

Dear Mr. and Mrs. Robins,

Thank you for the kind invitation to your dinner and dance for Graciella Elyse on Saturday, April 5. Unfortunately, Alicia and I are unable to attend the event because we have our niece's birthday party that same day. Please tell Graciella congratulations, and we hope to see you all soon!

With sincerest regrets,

Roberto Sullivan

Business-related Letter of Regret

Dear Anthony:

Thank you for inviting me to speak at the "Moving Forward" symposium in February. I am honored that you thought of me as a possible speaker. Unfortunately, I will be traveling most of February and cannot be a part of this year's program. Please let me know if there is any other assistance that I might be able to provide, or if I can suggest another colleague who might be available to present. Please do not hesitate to call me at 202-555-9984 to discuss.

Kindest regards,

Chantal Burnhardt

Chantal Burnhardt

Burnhardt, Murray, and Zink Associates

———— **USEFUL WORDS AND PHRASES** ————

Thank you for the invitation.

I am writing to accept your invitation to ___.

I am confirming ___.

I am honored you thought of me for ___.

I look forward to ___.

We are happy to share this occasion with you.

I regret to inform you that I will be unable to attend ___.

Thank you for including us.

Tips

Do

- ✉ thank the person for the invitation.
- ✉ respond in the time requested.
- ✉ reiterate the arrangements.
- ✉ use the active voice.
- ✉ sign your letter in pen.
- ✉ follow up on the arrangements if the situation is business-related.

Don't

- ✉ use a forceful tone.
- ✉ be afraid to ask for qualifying or additional information if the situation warrants it.

TOASTS AND CONGRATULATIONS

Toasts and congratulations are similar in that they both serve to honor the recipient. Though toasts are of the oral tradition, congratulations can be verbal or written. For toasts, it often helps the person giving the toast to write it down first. This is a good idea, for it may save the person giving the toast (and the people being toasted) from potential embarrassment.

Toasts should be brief. Nobody wants to hear a soliloquy of Shakespearean lengths during a toast. After all, the event is about the guest of honor, not the person giving the toast. You are not Hamlet. A good rule of thumb is don't let your toast last longer than the ice in your glass. You want your audience to remember what you said, not how long it took you to say it.

When preparing and making your toast or congratulations, you want to avoid telling personal stories about the person unless it is a story that shows the person in the best light. All toasts and congratulations should be sincere and from the heart. Keep in mind that a good toast should match the occasion.

Newlyweds drink to a new beginning, while a couple celebrating 50 years together drinks to the lifetime of beginnings they've shared. Graduates drink to the challenge of work, while retirees drink to the challenge of avoiding it. A birthday toast counts the days that have passed, while a good-bye toast counts the days until we meet again. Your goal is to mark the occasion, no matter what it might be.

If you're in the dilemma of having been asked to give a toast but don't think that you can present the person in the best light, you should either find something kind to say or turn the task over to someone who can. The only people who cannot turn toasting responsibilities over to another person, however, are the best man and maid- or matron-of-honor for a wedding.

Written congratulations can be used in conjunction with a milestone event, such as a graduation, retirement, or promotion. They can also be used in situations where you have learned about such an event after the fact and wish to express your joy at the person's achievement.

When preparing your toasts and congratulations, start with phrases such as "Here's to…" and "May…" These are excellent ways to start a simple sentiment for good fortune and honoring the individuals being toasted or congratulated. When starting a toast or congratulation this way, you can easily follow the opening with the hopes and wishes for the honored person or people. If choosing to start with a short story or joke, you would end your toast with the "Here's to…" and "May…" phrases. You can also choose short, traditional or cultural sayings, such as *"Mazel Tov,"* *"L'Chaim,"* or *"¡Salud!"*

You may also use religious passages or blessings if the toasts or congratulations are associated with a sacred event. For secular events, nondenominational religious passages can also be used, such as psalms. Short passages and excerpts from well-known texts, poems, and famous sayings or quotes can also be used, as well as funny sayings or quips about the ironies and truisms of life.

Toasts for Special Situations

When traveling abroad or making toasts in particularly delicate situations, be aware of the social customs of the group or culture you are with.

How to Write It

Written congratulations can be used to accompany a gift or to commemorate any significant life event, achievement, or milestone. Commercial greeting cards and personal stationery can be used for notes and letters of congratulations in personal situations. In business situations, both letterhead and commercial greeting cards are acceptable. Again, write from the heart and be sincere. Use the active or passive voice. Format your note in semi-block format, including your address, the date, and the recipient's address. Start by offering congratulations, making sure to include what you are congratulating them for. Include well wishes, such as for continued success, a long life together, or happiness.

In the end, the goal of both toasts and congratulations are to share sentiments for good health, wealth, success, and longevity, and to praise the honoree's accomplishments and goals and revel in their happiness.

Letter of Congratulations

Dear Angela,

I heard about the great news of you passing the Boards. I am so proud of you, but I know it cannot compare to how proud you are of this wonderful achievement, especially after such hard work. Congratulations, and may you have many more successes and blessings throughout your medical career!

With love,
Aunt Margaret

Letter of Congratulations

Dear Greg and Jane,

Let me begin by saying congratulations on your recent engagement! I heard the news, and I am so excited for you both. How wonderful that you've found your soul mate, and I wish you both an eternity of wedded bliss.

All my love,
Christine Larson

———————— USEFUL WORDS AND PHRASES ————————

General Congratulations

It's true—good things do happen to great people!

Celebrating success! Celebrating YOU!
Congratulations.

You are proof that dreams and possibilities are
endless when you believe in yourself.

Thank you for letting me share your joy!
Happiness shared is delight doubled.

Enjoy the love, laughter, and limelight
that is yours today.

May the happiness you're feeling today
go on and on and on!

Bells! Whistles! Fireworks! Well done!

Envisioning a dream is easy.
Seeing it through is not!

I'm overjoyed! It couldn't have
happened to a nicer person.

Three cheers from me to you on
your triumphant day!

I'm so happy for you. You deserve
nothing but the best.

No one deserves success more than you!

—✦—

Whatever you've been doing, keep doing it!

—✦—

I'm delighted about your news!
You truly earned this success.

—✦—

You deserve a round of applause
for a job well done!

Graduation

A cap. A gown. A diploma.
A whole new chapter in the story of you.
Congratulations!

—✦—

Wishing you adventure, success, and happiness
for all your tomorrows.

—✦—

May I make an educated guess?
You're the brightest and the best!

—✦—

We are so proud of all your accomplishments—
in the past and, especially, today.

—✦—

I'm so pleased for you! Now it's time to show
the world how you shine!

New Job, Promotions, and Retirement

You're a success looking for a chance to happen!
Congratulations on the new job!

—✦—

You've always been one step above the rest.
Good luck with your promotion.

New Job, Promotions, and Retirement (continued)

A new job, new friends,
new challenges—good luck!

Business brought us together, but
friendship has kept us close.
Here's to you, a wonderful associate and friend!

I always knew you'd go far—clearly, I'm not the
only one to recognize this!

You've helped your family grow and prosper,
now it's time to relax and enjoy the results.

Now it's time to really work—work hard at
enjoying life, that is!

Engagements, Weddings, and Anniversaries

What greater joy can there be for two
souls than to know
they are destined to be together?
Congratulations!

I'm so glad to hear that you're tying the knot!

Sparkling stone. Sparkling future.
Congratulations.

Life looks kindly on those who love and bestows
special blessings on those who join their hearts.

Here comes the bride! Happy engagement!

May today be the beginning of
a lifetime of beautiful days.

I'm so glad the two of you found each other.
May you never be lost again.

May your love grow with each passing day as you create
the life of your dreams.

A wedding day begins with the beautiful
sunrise of joyful anticipation. May it end
with the glorious sunset of fulfilled promises.

It is not enough to wish you happiness
in your life together.
I wish you a lifetime of days even
happier than today.

May your wedding day be just the beginning
of a new life overflowing with warmth,
laughter, connection, friendship, hope, and love.

May this couple forever be blessed with
all that makes them happiest!

Nothing is better than good old-fashioned love.
May yours see a ripe old age.

Here's to happiness: May it fill your life always!

May your love begin with "Once upon a time…"
and end with "happily every after."
Best wishes to you both on your wedding day.

——— USEFUL WORDS AND PHRASES (continued) ———

Engagements, Weddings, and Anniversaries (continued)

It's a day you'll remember forever.
Treasure it as I treasure both of you.

Let love lead the way through your life together.

May every tomorrow be twice as sunny and sweet
as all the days that came before.

Wishing you more love with every year you share.

The best way to enjoy life is to savor
the passing of time.
Let's celebrate another year together.

Your life together is an inspiration.
Happy anniversary!

The honeymoon still isn't over! Happy anniversary.

To a couple who have always made love and
marriage look so easy and natural. You two are
the greatest—a perfect match!

May your lives continue to be blessed by love.

It's hard enough to find love, but the
two of you found the miracle of true love.
Here's to many more beautiful years together!

Expecting a Baby and Births

I heard you've got a special delivery on
the way. Congratulations!

⚬+⚬

Your baby is very lucky:
What better parents than you!

⚬+⚬

Babies are little miracles with a whole lot of "kick."
Congratulations on your pregnancy.

⚬+⚬

A few months from now you'll learn that
you *can* do three things at once and that
moms really do have eyes
in the back of their heads!

⚬+⚬

Wishing you a happy, healthy bundle of love!

⚬+⚬

May your new baby bless your life
with joy and happiness.

⚬+⚬

A baby is God's way of telling us
hope is alive and well.

⚬+⚬

May today be the beginning of a
lifetime of beautiful days.

⚬+⚬

How wonderful that you're adding
more love to the world.

⚬+⚬

Take care of yourself, and let God do the rest.
Congratulations on your miracle from above.

⚬+⚬

May you savor the sweet joys of parenthood.

Expecting a Baby and Births (continued)

The sounds of baby feet will soon
fill your home with unimaginable
love and infectious laughter. Enjoy!

When a child is born, parents are too.
Congratulations on all of your birthdays!

May God bless and keep that little
miracle of yours.

May your new little one be as healthy
and happy as
he [or she] is beautiful!

What could be nicer than a new
baby to love? Congratulations!

A baby is life's greatest blessing.

Ribbons and bows and sweet baby toes.
Congratulations on the birth of
your daughter [or son]!

Baby girls [or boys] bring
the best life has to give.

May your new baby boy [or girl] open your eyes
to all that's beautiful in life.

Tips

Do

- ✉ write out your toast or congratulations if you will be speaking them.
- ✉ be sincere.
- ✉ write and speak from the heart.
- ✉ tell short stories that show the person or people in the best light.
- ✉ use congratulations for any occasion worth celebrating, especially milestones.

Don't

- ✉ let the toast last longer than the ice in your glass.
- ✉ tell embarrassing or negative personal stories.
- ✉ be afraid to use humor in your toast or congratulations.
- ✉ be afraid to use cultural phrases and religious or spiritual passages when appropriate.

CHAPTER
3
General Social Correspondence

L ETTERS. NOBODY SEEMS TO WRITE them anymore—at least not the kind that people actually want to read. We get letters offering new products, deals, and credit cards. We get letters requesting money, but when do we actually receive a personal letter from a friend or family member? Why not send someone a letter? Maybe someone you haven't seen or spoken to in a while, or maybe to tell someone that you miss them or that you're thinking of them. Sure, you could pick up the phone, but you know what may happen—the endless game of phone tag, or trying to catch up while doing something else, or yelling at the kids to stop fighting.

SOCIAL LETTERS

A quick letter or note just to say, "Hi, I'm thinking of you" is a great way to brighten someone's day—your best man, your maid of honor, or those great friends you were so close to but who are now sidetracked by responsibilities of work and family. We just don't have the same kind of time to spend with these old friends anymore because of other priorities or maybe geographical distance.

I know, you're thinking "What about e-mail?" We'll get to e-mail later, because this is something entirely different. Not everyone checks e-mail regularly, and with most of us having more than one e-mail account and all of them with spam and junk-mail filters, there's no guarantee they will receive your e-mail or have a chance to read it. But a letter with an address and a stamp on it—that's another story. Everyone gets the mail. The U.S. Postal Service has a pretty good track record, so sending "snail mail" is still reliable. Chances are the person you write to will be so happy to get something in the mail that's not a bill, a solicitation, or a promotional flyer that they'll want to open it right away.

Your letter doesn't have to be a long one. You don't need to tell your entire life story since the last time you saw each other. You can even use a greeting card to prompt you. There are a lot of "thinking of you" and nonromantic "missing you" cards on the market. There are also blank cards with great images that may be relevant to your personal history together. You could write inside the card itself—especially if it's blank—or you can use your note stationery and write a short letter yourself. You can also use special events, such as a birthday or anniversary of an event you shared together, as a reason to write. In the end, you really don't need a reason at all. Old friends and family members will be delighted to get this random act of kindness from someone special—you!

Complementary Closings

A complementary closing is the last line of a letter before your name and signature. Examples of complementary closings are:

- ✆ Thanks again!
- ✆ Hope to see you soon.
- ✆ Take care!
- ✆ Love,
- ✆ Best wishes,

How to Write It

Social letters can be handwritten or typed. Using semi-block format, begin with your name and address, the date, and the recipient's name and address. However, including addresses for social correspondence is optional. Start with "Dear [person's name]" followed by a comma. Start the first paragraph with something like "How are you?" and then tell the person why you are writing and what made you think of them. Maybe share personal stories and anecdotes. Your letter can be in the active voice or the passive voice, but keep the tone conversational. Invite the person to write back, and include a complementary closing followed by your name and signature.

Letter to an Old Friend

Dear Beth,

I was at the store today picking up some things for the kids. I turned down the wrong aisle and ended up in the card aisle, where I saw this card. It made me think of you immediately and how we used to go "shopping" in each other's closets when we were sick of our own. I hope you get the same chuckle out of it that I did!

How is everyone? The kids must be getting big! I can't believe it's been so long since we saw each other. Things here are well. The major news to report is that Melissa lost her front teeth. She's been trying to gross out her baby brother by sticking her tongue in the space where they used to be. Sound familiar?

I'm going to keep this short, but I hope to hear from you soon. Kisses all around!

Love,

Sandy

Letter to a Family Member

Marian Westfield
7447 Maple Street, Apt. 7F
Jacksonville, FL 32099

Dear Aunt Marian,

How are you? I wanted to write a quick note to say "hello" and to let you know I'm thinking of you. I know we don't get to see each other very often, but you are always in my thoughts and heart. Peter hopes to see you in the summer again, and he still talks about the fun he had at your house during our last visit—especially playing with Snowpuff. He calls all cats Snowpuff now. It's terribly cute, but it always warrants an explanation to new people. I've enclosed a couple of recent pictures of little Peter for you. You'll be amazed at how much he has grown. He has locks of curls just like cousin Jeff—it's uncanny! I guess they skipped me and went straight to Peter.

I hope you enjoy the pictures. We will check our calendars and plan another family trip to see you soon. Of course, you are always welcome at our home as well!

With love,

Dawn

See how easy that was? Sometimes a few paragraphs and a sweet anecdote or two are all you need for an uplifting note to brighten anyone's day.

──────── **USEFUL WORDS AND PHRASES** ────────

To have a friend is to have everything.

I was just thinking of you.

You're like family to me. Thanks for being such a great friend.

Friendship is a privilege—I feel privileged to
have you as a friend.

The echo of your laughter brightens my day—I miss you!

Just thinking of you makes me happy.

A friend is a guardian angel in disguise.
Thanks for always watching out for me.

To have one true friend is lucky.
To have a friend like you is a miracle.

Good friends are the rare jewels of life—
difficult to find and impossible to replace.

Just the thought of you makes me feel closer to home.

We've played roles in many chapters of each other's lives.
Thank you for being such a true and faithful friend.

I've been thinking about you so much
that I feel like we're together again.

If absence makes the heart grow fonder, you must
be my fondest friend! Please keep in touch.

Through your letters, I hear your laughter. Please write soon.

Tips

Do

- ✉ be sincere.
- ✉ be conversational and light.
- ✉ share something personal, but also invite a dialogue.
- ✉ encourage the person to write back.
- ✉ use the active or passive voice.

Don't

- ✉ bring up something negative.

VACATION LETTERS

A fun thing to do while you are traveling is to send postcards or short letters from afar to friends and family back home. It lets them know you are thinking of them, even if you're on vacation. You don't need to do this for a short weekend trip unless you've gone to an exotic or unusual location, but remember that your postcard may arrive long after you have returned home.

The body of a postcard or a short letter doesn't need to be long. There isn't a lot of space on postcards anyway, so you need to be brief or write small. (Just don't write so small that the person reading it needs a magnifying glass.) Keep in mind that postcards will probably get read by anyone who handles them, so choose your words carefully and use decorum. Write to your family and friends or close coworkers just to say a quick "hi" and to share some of the sights you've seen or something interesting about the trip. Don't use postcards and notes from afar as a dig—as in "Ha, ha! I'm on vacation and you're not!" Be sincere and light. When writing to loved ones back home, don't forget to tell them you miss them and love them.

If you're on a cruise or staying in a hotel, it is perfectly acceptable to use the stationery that is provided in your room or suite. As tempting as it may be, do not take the stationery back home with you to use as your own stationery. Besides, you have that lovely stationery wardrobe at home anyway, and that's what it's there for—your correspondence when you're at home.

———— USEFUL WORDS AND PHRASES ————

Wishing you were here.

The miles between us are nothing because
you're always in my heart.

I hope this note finds you with a happy heart.

Out of sight, out of mind? Not a chance!

I know this would be a perfect
spot for your next vacation.

I wish I could share this experience with you.

If wishing could make it so, you'd be with me right now.
Wishing you were here.

We may be far apart, but you're always in my thoughts.

"Wish you were here" just doesn't
express how much I miss you!

You're there. I'm here. We're nuts!

Sending good old-fashioned hugs and kisses with good
old-fashioned snail mail. Wish you were here!

You won't believe the sights! I'm taking lots
of pictures, and I can't wait to share them with you.

Tips

Do

- ✉ be brief, especially on postcards.
- ✉ use the active voice.
- ✉ make a sincere statement about missing them or wishing they were there.
- ✉ share something about your vacation experience.
- ✉ remember that you don't need a reason to write.

Don't

- ✉ take the stationery from your hotel or cruise ship.
- ✉ write anything on a postcard you don't want others to read.
- ✉ rib the person for not being on vacation or try to make them jealous.

LOVE LETTERS

What could be more delightful than receiving a letter from your sweetheart? Writing one to your sweetheart. Love letters seem to be making a comeback, especially after the success of films such as *The Notebook, The Lake House,* and *Love in the Time of Cholera.* Love letters, however, arc so personal that you have to be careful when you write them.

Avoid the temptation to include anything in your love letter you would not want someone other than your sweetie to read, just in case the letter gets into the wrong hands. Hopefully your significant other will have the discretion not to share the contents of your letters with others. As a token of affection, a love letter is a private communication *entres nous*—just between us.

Love letters can help brighten, spark, and enliven a relationship, especially since many couples today are separated by hundreds or thousands of miles for weeks or months at a time because of military service, work, or school. Love letters don't need to be reserved for Valentine's Day (February 14) or Sweetest Day (the third Saturday in October). They aren't only for those couples who are geographically separated, either. You can send one to your spouse or boyfriend or girlfriend even when you live together. In your love letters, be sincere and speak from the heart.

The Greeting Card Holiday

According to American Greetings, more than 190 million cards are exchanged on Valentine's Day. American Greetings alone generates annual net sales of approximately $1.7 billion, which includes greeting cards, e-cards, and other greeting products.

Often, a love letter can do what spoken words cannot. You don't need to sound as lovesome as poet Elizabeth Barrett Browning, but you can still wear your heart on a sheet of paper—even if you cannot wear it on your sleeve. Like with other forms of social correspondence, love letters are also a sweet addition to a greeting card. They can be short, but you want the person reading them to feel the same level of excitement and anticipation when opening and reading your letter as they do when they're with you. As with any letter, consider your audience. If your sweetheart isn't one for flowery phrases, skip them. Though the steamy love letter is probably not a good idea for new relationships, vague allusions to passion might be—especially if you are certain that no one else will read it. Beyond the standard rules of letter writing, there are no rules for sharing your love and sense of passion in a love letter. The only limits are the boundaries of your unique relationship.

How to Write It

Start by examining your relationship and your feelings about your significant other. Use the active voice and tell your sweetheart why you love them and what it is about them that makes you happy and in love. It's that simple. The format can be formal or informal, but it should be handwritten because it helps express the deep personal nature of the letter.

Love Letter

> Dearest Meghan,
>
> Everything about you captivates me. When you look at me, I find it hard to speak and hard to think. I get lost in your eyes and in your laughter. With you, my soul leaps. I feel so special and honored that I am yours.
>
> With all my love,
>
> *Francis*

Sometimes that's really all you need to write in a love letter to express your feelings. It doesn't have to sound like a romance novel, and it doesn't have to include every romantic thought you've ever had about your sweetheart.

Tips

Do

- ☒ be sincere about your feelings.
- ☒ be brief and to the point.
- ☒ use the active voice.
- ☒ remember that there are no limits except for the boundaries of your unique relationship.

Don't

- ☒ put anything in your letter that you wouldn't want someone else to read.
- ☒ limit writing love letters for holidays and special occasions.

————— USEFUL WORDS AND PHRASES —————

You touch my life in a million wonderful ways.

I was just counting my blessings,
and you came to mind.

My thoughts, my heart, and my love are with you.

I am so thankful for the gift of you.

You're forever on my mind and in my heart. I love you!

My heart beats *because* of you. My life *is* you.

Our relationship is a blessing. Please know that I love you.

My world is brighter now that you're in it.

Anywhere with you is a wonderful place to be.

Without your love, I wouldn't be the person I am today.

I'll never grow tired of telling you how much I love you.

Love shared is love multiplied.
I want you to know I love you.

I don't know where I would be without you,
and I'm happy that I don't have to find out.

Our love isn't a fairy tale. It's better—it's real.

Life without you? Not a chance.
Life with you? Endless romance.

ALL IS FAIR IN LOVE AND WAR—
THE "DEAR JOHN" LETTER

Paul Simon once sang, "there are 50 ways to leave your lover."
One thing he didn't mention was *writing* your lover about it. It's
not a nice thing to do, but sometimes you find yourself in a situation where you need to.

"Dear John" or breakup letters should be used as a last resort and
when there is absolutely no other way to dissolve the relationship.
Be sincere and direct but don't be mean. Don't use your "Dear
John" letter as a forum for telling your former love about all their
worst traits and habits. You want to break things off as smoothly
as possible, not wound your former lover or give them a reason to
retaliate.

Be sensitive to their feelings and acknowledge that you are sorry
for the pain this may cause them. Keep the letter short and to the
point. As described in previous chapters, a letter should not be
longer than two pages. This is especially important if it's a "Dear
John" letter.

After you write your "Dear John" letter and before you send
it, sleep on it for a day or two. Then read it again and remove
anything you think would be severely hurtful or could be misconstrued as a way out of breaking up. Try to put yourself in the
recipient's shoes—if you received your own "Dear John" letter,
would it cause you to react in an irrational way? If so, rewrite the
letter.

How to Write It

Similar to love letters, you should start by examining your relationship and your feelings. It is best to handwrite the letter, unless
the emotional gravity of the situation makes your penmanship
difficult to read. Use semi-block format. Be candid but sincere.
Begin the letter explaining why you are writing it. Be clear about
the intentions of the letter. End the letter on a positive tone and
wish the person well. Do not use "Love," for your complementary
closing, as that will only confuse the reader.

Breakup Letter

Dear John,

Writing this is extremely difficult and painful for me. I have tried to talk to you about our relationship, but to no avail. It is clear to me that we want very different things and that we are on different paths. You have been a great friend, and we have had wonderful and happy times together. But those happy times have given way to a relationship that is stagnant and unfulfilling—I think for both of us. This is beyond a temporary setback or a "bump in the road," and I have decided that it is best that we no longer see each other. It will not be easy for either of us.

Know that you will always have a special place in my heart and that I will cherish the good times we have had. Perhaps in time, as we both heal and grow, we may be friends again. But for now, I know that is not possible because it will be too easy to fall into our old patterns. I am sorry for any pain this may cause you, I just need you to understand.

Sincerely,

Mary

———— USEFUL WORDS AND PHRASES ————

I am sorry to do this in writing instead of in person.

Though we have had some wonderful times…

Always know that you hold a special
place in my heart.

I can no longer be a part of this relationship.

Please know that I don't hate you.

I feel it's time for both of us to move on.

We are not in the same place with
this relationship anymore.

I wish you a lifetime of happiness. You deserve it.

Perhaps, in time, we will get past this and enjoy being in
each other's lives again.

I sincerely hope that one day we will be friends.

I am writing this letter because
you deserve to know exactly how I feel.

Please know that our relationship was filled with
many happy memories.

I do not blame you for being confused about
the way I feel, and I hope this letter helps.

I hope you cherish the good times
we've had. I know I will.

Tips

Do

- ☒ be candid, polite, and sincere.
- ☒ write in the active voice, even if you are writing about past events.
- ☒ sleep on the letter for one or two days, and reread it before sending it.
- ☒ be specific about why you are breaking up.
- ☒ explain why you're writing them instead of telling them in person. Some people may be confused about receiving a breakup in writing.
- ☒ use specific examples if necessary and if it would help the person better understand.

Don't

- ☒ be mean or intentionally hurtful.
- ☒ send a "Dear John" letter unless you absolutely intend to break up with the person.
- ☒ use the breakup letter as a way to tell the person about their negative traits.
- ☒ make the letter all about you. Acknowledge the pain you may be causing them, not just the pain you feel.
- ☒ close with "Love," or "Yours Truly," or any similar closing phrase that might give the reader a mixed message.
- ☒ only write "it's over" and leave it at that. Explain why.
- ☒ use curse words.

HATE MAIL—LETTERS WRITTEN IN ANGER

Like "Dear John" letters, hate mail is emotionally charged. Letters written in anger can be therapeutic for the writer. You can get all your rage and fury out on paper and avoid other ways of mismanaging your temper or mishandling a situation. Hate mail and angry letters should rarely be sent. Go ahead, though. Write the letter. Allow it to be long and ramble on to get out all your frustration. Do not, however, send it. Like with "Dear John" letters, it is important to let the letter rest—put it down and sleep on it for a day or two. Then take the letter out and reread it. Try not to get angry all over again, just consider why you were angry in the first place. If there are key issues or topics that need to be addressed, keep those and delete any personal attacks or curse words. Then go back over the key points and try to address them clearly and succinctly so that your letter is not longer than two pages. Consider how you would feel if you received such a letter and give that same courtesy to the person you are writing. Remember that they may not know why you are angry with them or that they have done something so displeasing that you need to write them about it. If after you have edited your original letter and it turns out that you are willing to speak to the person, use the letter as a guide for talking to them. If you are still too upset to talk to the person, let the letter sit for another day and repeat the process until you are certain that this is what you want to say. If you still need to send the letter, go ahead and send it. But be prepared for the consequences, and don't forget to destroy the original rant.

How to Write It

Many of the same rules apply for angry letters as for "Dear John" letters. Think about why you are angry. Use the active voice, be direct, candid, and sincere. Do not be mean or rude. Use the semi-block format for your typed or handwritten letter. If you are writing a family member or close friend, it may be a good idea to handwrite the letter because it will be more personal. Remember that the reader may not realize you are angry, so be sure to explain why you are angry or disappointed. If there is an action that you need the reader to do, tell them so in a firm but polite manner. Use terms such as "I feel" and "I believe" when describing what the person did to make you angry. You can close your letter with "Sincerely," or "Respectfully," depending on the circumstance.

Angry Letter

Dear Samantha,

I am writing you because I have to get something off my chest. At this point, I am not sure if I can discuss it with you in person yet.

I am really irritated by the way you constantly flirt with my boyfriend. We've known each other for many years now, and you are a great friend. But whenever all of us are together and there is a guy present—even if the guy is with someone else—you turn into a completely different person.

I am confident in my relationship with Sean, so it's not that you are a threat, just a distraction. Guys can't seem to resist your hair twirling, eye batting, constant touching, and other flirtations that, in any other situation, you would never do. I need you to stop. Whether you stop doing it with others, I don't care. But when it comes to Sean, please stop. You can be friendly, but the overly flirtatious behavior with him has to end.

I know that you are a caring and true friend, so I know you will be able to do this small thing for me. I sincerely hope that you value our friendship as much as I do and will understand where I'm coming from.

Sincerely yours,

Tammy

———— **USEFUL WORDS AND PHRASES** ————

I am sorry to do this in writing instead of in person.

This is difficult to say, so I am writing you instead.

I want to tell you that something has been bothering me.

Please understand that I don't hate you.

I truly value our friendship, but there's something
I need to get off my chest.

When you [action], it makes me feel [emotion].

I need you to understand how I feel
about what has happened.

Tips ————————————————

Do

- ✉ be candid, direct, and polite.
- ✉ write in the active voice, even if you are writing about past events.
- ✉ let the letter sit and reread it before sending it. Rewrite the letter if necessary.
- ✉ be specific about why you are angry.
- ✉ tell the reader if there is an action you need from them.

Don't

- ✉ be mean.
- ✉ send a letter that is longer than two pages.
- ✉ use the letter as a way to tell the person about all their faults.

APOLOGIES

In 1976, Elton John sang, "Sorry seems to be the hardest word." But it doesn't have to be. Apologies can go a long way to mend a relationship that has been fractured. That's not to say that it will heal everything, but at the very least, it will let the person you've offended know you acknowledge that you have hurt them—whether intentionally or accidentally.

There are two kinds of apologies. The first kind is the truly sincere apology, where you are as devastated for hurting someone as they are hurt. Second is the the social apology, where you realize that it is best to keep peace by extending the olive branch and acknowledging your infraction, whether or not you thought you were wrong.

The key in an apology is realizing that it is not about you. It's about the person to whom you are apologizing. In some instances, you can offer ways to make amends. Or better yet, just do it. Do not go into writing an apology letter expecting immediate forgiveness or reconciliation. Depending on how deep the wound is—whether real or imagined, metaphoric, physical, or emotional—it will determine if and when forgiveness is granted. Once you've extended the apology, the outcome is up to the recipient. Consider the kind of apology you would want were the shoe on the other foot. Be sincere, even if you're writing a social apology. Most people who know you well will read right through insincerity.

How to Write It

Use personal stationery or a greeting card to handwrite your apology. Use semi-block format. Keep the apology brief but directly say what you are apologizing about. That way, the recipient will know that you realize what you did and that what you did hurt or offended them. Use the active voice and, where possible, offer to make up for your actions. Close your letter by restating your apology along with "Sincerely yours," followed by your signature.

Sincere Apology (in response to Tammy's letter written in anger)

Dear Tammy,

I got your letter. I'm writing because after reading your letter, I figure you are still too upset to talk to me right now. I was wondering why we hadn't seen each other lately. I had no idea I've been causing you so much distress.

Please know that I would never intentionally do anything to come between you and Sean, and I am so very sorry that my behavior seemed inappropriate. I thought that I was being fun and friendly, and I guess I went over the line. When I think about it, I probably would be angry too if the tables were turned.

I'd hate to think that I'd done something to cause a rift in our relationship when we've been such great friends for so long and have been through so much together. I hope you can accept my sincere apology.

Please give me a call when you're ready and maybe we can get together—just us girls. Remember that I love you always!

Very sincerely,

Samantha

From Samantha's letter, you can tell she was caught off guard not only by Tammy's letter, but also by the fact that she was doing something that hurt her friend. She responds by acknowledging her friend's anger and what she did to offend Tammy, and is sincere in doing so. She also offers a way to mend the situation but gives Tammy enough space to reconnect in her own time. Given how upset Tammy was, chances are that a letter of apology is not what she will be expecting. By receiving an apology letter from Samantha that is sincere and acknowledges her need for space in dealing with the issue, it may even soften her.

Social Apology

Dear Mr. Beck,

I am writing you to sincerely apologize for when my friend Mike broke the windshield of your car when we were playing baseball at my house on Saturday. I realize that since Mike was my guest, I am responsible for his actions. I hope that by offering to mow your lawn for the next three weekends that will make up for the cost of a new windshield. I sincerely hope you accept my apology and that you are no longer upset with my parents or me.

Sincerely, your neighbor,

Billy Adams

In this letter of apology, Billy probably doesn't think he should have to do anything to make up for something that he didn't actually do. But he also has an end goal—he doesn't like that there is negativity between his family and his neighbor, so he offers an apology and a method of recompense.

Even if Mr. Beck doesn't take Billy up on his offer, Mr. Beck will probably be touched that Billy thought about it—even if it was prompted by his parents.

USEFUL WORDS AND PHRASES

I am sorry to do this in writing instead of in person.

I didn't realize how much I hurt you.

I'm sorry that I hurt you.

I apologize for causing you pain.

I promise I will try to do better.

I sincerely hope you know this was not intentional.

I hope you can forgive me.

Our friendship means the world to me, and
I hope this does not come between us.

Please accept this heartfelt apology.

You have a special gift for listening
with your heart. I hope we can
eventually get past this.

When I count my blessings, our friendship
tops the list. Nothing would mean
more than your forgiveness.

This has been a learning experience for me,
and I hope I never have to repeat it.

Tips

Do

- ✉ acknowledge the person's feelings.
- ✉ directly apologize for what you have done or how you have hurt them.
- ✉ be sincere and write from the heart.
- ✉ offer to make up for your actions if the situation warrants it.
- ✉ ask for forgiveness if the situation warrants it.

Don't

- ✉ discount the person's feelings.
- ✉ make excuses for yourself or your actions.
- ✉ make false promises.
- ✉ write an angry or hurtful letter as a response.

SYMPATHY LETTERS

When just the right words are needed, it's often the hardest to find them. Loss and grief are universal emotions, but they are also very personal. People sometimes wonder whether it is better to not say anything so as not to further upset the person in need of sympathy. But by acknowledging another's pain or difficulty, you can help them work through it. It also lets the person know that he or she is not alone, and at the very least, that someone is thinking of them, praying for them, or sending them well wishes.

Similar to letters of apology, think of the kinds of things you would want to hear from others. Remember that offering sympathy is not about you, it is about the recipient. However, it's good to be mindful of the person's personality and how they tend to handle things. If, for example, they tend to be vague or introverted about personal issues, then you should be vague, too. For instance, when discussing cancer, some people say, "the C word" instead of calling it by name. Therefore, if they are grieving for someone who has lost the battle, you shouldn't say, "I'm sorry Jack's cancer took its toll." Instead, say something more sensitive such as, "I am sorry for your loss." However, if they are open about sharing, be just as forthright in your choice of words. Know that as long as what you write is sincere, it is bound to be appreciated.

Many think that the only time to offer sympathy is for death or grave illness. But life's journey has many ups and downs, and the low points are when people need the support of their friends and family to get through them. These periods include job loss, divorce or separation, coping with illness, a bad breakup, or any other negative or unpleasant situation. But don't let this list limit you. If you feel the need to express your caring, empathy, or sympathy to someone you care about, go ahead. A sympathy letter can be a simple random act of kindness that elevates the spirits of someone who is down.

A sympathy letter should acknowledge the person's emotional state, whether it is pain, anguish, sorrow, or anger. Share your empathy—your deep understanding of the situation—with a personal anecdote. If you haven't personally been in that same situation, and therefore cannot add a personal anecdote, explain how you can only begin to imagine what it would be like to be in their situation.

Offer emotional assistance when realistically possible and appropriate. Don't pledge support that you have no intention, desire, or ability to uphold should the person accept your offer. This may sound harsh. Some people think, "Well everyone knows that it's just what you say, but nobody ever takes you up on it." But that's not necessarily true. A person who is in pain just might reach out to grab that emotional lifeline you've offered, and in writing no less. To suggest that there is no limit to your time or availability is insincere and unfair to them and to you. Instead, you can add words of encouragement and hope that can help the person through the difficult period they are in.

A Quick Guide to Everyday Punctuation and Symbols

Punctuation is the tool for conveying emotion, inserting breaks or pauses, and determining possession. Using correct punctuation in your writing is key; otherwise your intended meaning may not be presented, or you may confuse the reader. Here are some basic punctuation marks and their uses. Some will seem obvious, others may not.

.   period: at the end of a sentence.

?   question mark: at the end of a question.

!   exclamation point: indicates a higher level of emotion than a simple statement.

,   comma: indicates a series of things in a short list that does not require bulleting; used to make a short pause; used in separating numbers 1,000 and above.

;   semicolon: separates two independent clauses that could stand alone were they not in one sentence or thought. It is also used to separate a series of longer items in a list.

'   apostrophe: in contractions or as a placeholder for a missing letter, number, or series of letters or numbers; to indicate possession by someone or something. For example, Mike's house or the book's pages.

()   parentheses: to separate an interjection or secondary thought into a sentence.

" "   quotation marks: when quoting or citing a person. In less formal situations, they can be used to indicate the equivalent of the phrases "so called" or "assumed."

:   colon: used to offset a list or a group of items belonging to the same category.

-    hyphen or dash: a joiner to make compound words, avoid ambiguity, or separate units contained in a group, such as in a telephone number.

$ dollar sign: used only when writing currency values; the word "dollar" should not appear with the dollar sign.

@   at sign: used only in an e-mail address. For any other uses, write out the word "at."

&   ampersand or "and" sign: avoid in writing as a substitute for the word "and," unless it is part of a title or name.

number or pound sign: should be avoided in writing unless you are indicating that someone needs to use that symbol. For example, dial 1–800–555–0000, then press #. Instead, write out or use the written abbreviations for "number" or "pound."

%   percent: may be used as its symbol or written out; assigns a value to percentages. For example, statistics would suggest that 50% of the population is male. However when using percent as a noun, write out the word. For example, twenty is what percent of 100?

Remembering people who have suffered a loss in the past is also important. Holidays, birthdays, and anniversaries can be difficult times for people who are in a state of distress. They are often reminders of what they have lost when it seems that everyone around them is filled with joy. In these situations, timing is critical. If you know that someone's birthday is approaching, make sure that you send your greeting so that it arrives on or before the person's birthday (or the birthday of the person who has died, if that is the case). Doing so will help the recipient through what may be a recurring period of difficulty and sadness. Christmas, Hanukkah, and Thanksgiving are critical periods. If the person is suffering from grief related to military service—their own or a loved one's, whether tragic injury or death—don't forget them on Memorial Day and Veteran's Day.

In her *Guide to Excruciatingly Correct Behavior*, Miss Manners gives examples of what not to say to the bereaved. This list can also include anyone who is in a state of despair, not just those who are mourning the death of a loved one. This list includes but is not limited to:

- ☞ It's all for the best.
- ☞ He [or she] wouldn't have wanted you to grieve.
- ☞ He [or she] wouldn't have wanted you to cry.
- ☞ Do you think you ought to be going about like this—so soon after ___?
- ☞ You can always have more children.
- ☞ You're young, smart, handsome [or pretty]. You can remarry.
- ☞ Don't you think it's too early to ___?
- ☞ At least you had many years together. It's not like what happened to me when ___.

The statements above should be avoided because most of them imply some unsolicited judgment about how the person is handling a tragedy. They may seem well intentioned, but they are in poor taste. Unless the person asks for your opinion, keep it to yourself. As in the last example, don't try to diminish their situation by talking about your own. That's not what is meant by the suggestion to empathize by showing you understand. The focus should be on the person in pain and not on you. Remember that sympathy is not about you. It's about the person in pain. You can offer the personal story as an anecdote to let them know that you

Greeting Cards

Greeting cards are everywhere. They exist for just about every occasion, but don't let the greeting card speak for you alone. Though greeting-card messages can be sincere, they can never fully convey your personal touch. Include a personal note written on the card (assuming space allows for it) or include a handwritten personal note on stationery.

can relate, but don't use their grief as a platform to discuss your own situation. The simple and correct way to approach it is to say, "I know what you're going through, and I've been through something similar." You can then offer your ear or shoulder for support with a statement such as, "If you want to talk or hear how I got through it, let me know. I'm here for you."

How to Write It

Sympathy letters should be handwritten on personal stationery or typed on personal letterhead. They can also be handwritten in a blank card or greeting card in addition to the sentiment printed in the card. Use semi-block format. The wording can be formal or informal and can be in the passive or active voice. Write from the heart. Start by acknowledging the person's grief, sorrow, or pain and how you learned about it. Express your sympathy next and offer words of kindness.

Death or Condolence

Dear Margaret,

I was so sorry to hear that your father had died, and I am sorry I could not attend the funeral. Your father was such a wonderful man, and I have such vivid memories of him coaching the girls' softball team. He was always so encouraging and hysterically funny. He could turn even the worst game into something positive.

I wish you much comfort, peace, and many happy memories of him to get you through this difficult time. My thoughts and prayers are with you and your family.

Your childhood friend,

Julia

Miscarriage

Dear Sandra,

Jack told me that you had a miscarriage fairly late in your pregnancy, and I am so sorry for your loss. I know how excited you and Jack were, and I also know what you are going through—Matthew and I were there a few years ago. If you need someone to talk to about it or just need some additional companionship during this difficult time, let me know and we can get together for tea. Matthew also offers the same for Jack, since it's not easy on the father's side either. I know that I could have called, but I wanted to write instead. Just know that you have a lot of support, and that you are in our thoughts and prayers.

Very sincerely,

Ellen

Divorce, Separation, or Breakup

Dear Jonah,

The second I heard from my sister that Julie left, I had to write. I can only imagine how hard it is, and how plans to build a life together are suddenly changed—especially after moving halfway across the country to do so. Please know that George and I are here for you to listen and to help the best way that we can. You have a lot of friends to support you through this difficult time. We will help you get through it so that you can have the happiness you deserve.

Sincerely,

Mary

Military-related

Dear Bill,

I've been thinking about Zach a lot lately. Perhaps it is because Memorial Day is approaching. I realize that this must be a difficult time for you and Margaret, and I wanted to share my thoughts of how proud I am of Zach for serving our country. Zach was always a fine boy, and you raised him to be such a good, upstanding man. I am sure that as a soldier, he was no less than a brilliant and true leader.

It is never easy to lose a child, and I am sure that though every day may get a bit easier, it can still be difficult. Please know that my thoughts and prayers are with you today and always. May the happy memories of Zach and your pride in him bring you continued comfort.

Fondly from your dear friend,

Larry

Anniversary of a Sad Event or Birthday of Deceased

Dear Marcia,

How are you? I just wanted to write to let you know that we're thinking of you. We know that this is a difficult time of year with Paul's birthday approaching for the first time since his death. Know that we love you very much and that you are always near in our hearts and thoughts, even if we are miles apart.

Lovingly,

Barbara

These letters are only a few examples of the types of letters you can write to convey sympathy. The possibilities are endless. No matter the situation, if you think someone could use a little sunshine on an otherwise dreary day, a letter of sympathy is the perfect way to do so. All you need is something to write about, something to write on, and something to write with.

Don't forget to be sincere and write from the heart. A simple sympathy letter to a friend, relative, or coworker takes very little time and effort, but it could mean the world to the recipient.

Tips

Do

- ✉ be sincere.
- ✉ briefly and in sensitive terms mention why you are offering sympathy.
- ✉ offer support when possible.
- ✉ share a personal anecdote about the deceased.
- ✉ remember those mourning or struck with grief at holidays, birthdays, and anniversaries.
- ✉ include inspirational words and hopeful sentiments.

Don't

- ✉ use the sympathy letter as a platform for rehashing your own personal tragedy.
- ✉ offer support if you are not able to follow through on your promise.
- ✉ offer unsolicited advice for how to get through it.
- ✉ be afraid to write a light-hearted letter of sympathy. Remember to consider your audience first.
- ✉ be afraid to offer prayers and other spiritual wisdom or phrases.

——— USEFUL WORDS AND PHRASES ———

It's hard to understand why people are taken
from us, but find comfort in knowing you
were a special part of a well-lived life.

Memories of love and friendship are treasures to
carry with you always.

When the Lord calls our loved ones home,
he leaves a gift of memories in exchange.
I'm here if you want to talk.

Take the lessons you've learned and the love you
shared, and turn it into knowledge for tomorrow.

No matter how alone you feel, you're not.
I'm here for you.

Don't dwell too long on what was or what
might have been; what will be is waiting.

You're in my thoughts every step of the way.

The toughest moments in life don't break us—they make us.

Take heart. Time will soften the edges
and ease your burden.

We hold you safe in our hearts at this time of sadness.

When your heart is empty, filling it with
happy memories can help.

I cannot take away your pain, but I can listen if
you want to talk about it.

A FEW MORE USEFUL TIPS FOR
GENERAL SOCIAL CORRESPONDENCE

- ☞ Handwrite your personal notes and letters when possible.
- ☞ Keep apology letters brief, but say directly what you are apologizing for.
- ☞ Don't let your letter run longer than two pages.
- ☞ In apologies and sympathy letters, avoid using them as a platform to tell your own sad tale.
- ☞ Be sincere, honest, and forthright.
- ☞ Write from the heart.
- ☞ Remember that you don't need a reason or a specific occasion to write to someone.
- ☞ Don't save condolences and sympathies for only when the tragedy occurrs.
- ☞ When sending emotionally charged letters, sleep on them for a day or two before, then reread and edit anything that could be hurtful before sending them.
- ☞ Acknowledge the person's situation and feelings when writing sympathy letters and apologies.
- ☞ Remember that letters are not about you. They are about the recipient.

GET-WELL-SOON LETTERS

Letters and short notes can lift someone's spirit when they're suffering or recovering from a prolonged illness, an accident, or a surgery. Whether the person is in the hospital or at home, an illness could mean many hours spent alone. People may not be themselves and may have limited capabilities. This can lead to feelings of sadness, grief, and depression. Even if you cannot visit them, a get-well-soon note is sometimes more appreciated and more helpful than flowers.

How to Write It

Your get-well-soon note should be handwritten on personal stationery or in a greeting card. Be sincere in your expression for the person's well-being and briefly let them know how you heard about their situation if they did not tell you themself. You may use either the active or passive voice. Similar to sympathy letters, do not use get-well notes as a platform to discuss your own ailments.

However, if you can appropriately offer genuine assistance—either emotionally or in person—go ahead. Also consider the personality of the person you're writing. Sometimes a humorous approach is the perfect way to bring a smile to someone's face.

Get-Well-Soon Letter

Dear Mitch,

I heard from my mother the other day that you recently had knee-replacement surgery. And to think, you were always the invincible one during all those years playing hockey together! Now we have something else in common. I've had a few issues with my knees as well, as I'm sure my mother told you. If you want to talk, don't hesitate to give me a call.

I am glad to hear that the surgery was a success, and I'm sure you'll be back on your feet (and probably back on the ice) in no time. Between Beth and Dr. Morris, you couldn't be in better hands. Wishing you a speedy recovery, and we'll have to see how that new knee of yours holds up on the ice the next time I'm in town!

Always and fondly,

Pete

——— USEFUL WORDS AND PHRASES ———

May the sun shine on your speedy recovery.

Get better soon—there is still much
joy ahead of you!

I'm sorry you've been under the weather.
I hope you'll be feeling sunny again soon!

We miss you when you're not here.
Here's wishing you a speedy recovery!

That was quite a scare! I'm so thankful
you're feeling stronger.

If there is anything I can do to make
you feel better, I'll feel better as well.

We all miss your smile, and hope
you'll feel better soon.

Hope you're feeling back on top
of the world soon!

I hope this card will brighten your day and
help you get better without delay.

Look on the bright side, at least you
get breakfast in bed!

Keep your chin up, your temperature
down, and get well soon.

Thinking of you as you recover, and sending
prayers to make you stronger.

The way you've handled what has been dealt
to you has been so inspiring. Your spirit has
shined through it all.

Tips

Do

- ⊠ be sincere and positive.
- ⊠ tell the person how you heard about the illness.
- ⊠ offer support when possible.
- ⊠ invite the person to contact you to talk if you have experienced something similar.
- ⊠ share a personal anecdote if warranted.
- ⊠ include inspirational words and hopeful sentiments.

Don't

- ⊠ use the get-well note as a platform for rehashing your own illness or surgery.
- ⊠ offer unsolicited advice for how to get through it.
- ⊠ be afraid to offer prayers and other spiritual wisdom or phrases.
- ⊠ be negative or pessimistic about the person's condition.

HOLIDAY LETTERS

Some people prepare for the holiday season months in advance. They purchase the packages of greeting cards that went on sale immediately after Christmas last year. They have their database of names and addresses ready to print labels the day after Thanksgiving and will start signing their cards soon after that. Others have chosen the family photo and have placed their order with a photo-processing company and all that's left to do is click, pay, and send. For others who want to spread the holiday cheer, there is the holiday letter, an increasingly popular end-of-year greeting that goes out to family and friends.

The holiday letter can be a thoughtful way to keep up with friends and family who you don't normally get to stay in touch with throughout the year. The holiday letter is one way to stay in contact that is more personal than a signed "Season's Greetings" card. On one hand, it eliminates the need to write personal notes in every single greeting card. Although that's a nice touch, writing personal notes on each one may take more time than you realistically have or when you have a list of hundreds of people who you wish to send your holiday greetings. You can, however, still write a personal note to selected people on your holiday letter.

Avoid sending the family holiday letter to business associates unless they are also close, personal friends. Business associates you do not know well may appreciate a holiday card, but when it comes to holiday letters, they may not be interested in your personal life or that your fifth grader won the school spelling bee. Also, be sure to mail your holiday letter early enough to avoid missing people who may be on vacation.

How to Write It

When writing the holiday letter, consider three things: timing, style, and audience. First, you want to ensure that your letter arrives on time for the holiday you are writing for. Hanukkah moves throughout the calendar each year, so pay close attention to that date. Kwanzaa is December 26 through January 1. While Christmas always falls on December 25, traditionally it is 12 days long; don't fret if the people on your list don't receive your letter by December 24. As long as it arrives before January 6 (Epiphany or Three Kings Day), you should be safe.

The U.S. Postal Service always posts the holiday mailing dates and times on its Web site and at physical post office locations to ensure proper holiday delivery. If in doubt, ask your mail carrier or an associate at the post office. People who live in rural areas and have mail pick-up service at their homes or businesses may also want to check on the mail availability and schedule during the holidays. In some areas you can schedule a pick-up by the U.S. Postal Service online at *www.usps.com*. If you are sending your letter electronically, avoid sending it the last two weeks of December and the first three days of January since this is when most people are on vacation. This is especially important for businesses—there is nothing worse than getting back to the office on January 2 only to spend the first half of your workday sorting through e-mails.

Second, consider your family or business style when writing your letter and then determine whether you want the letter to include images from family or business events, a border, or other decorative motifs. Create bullet points for topics you would like to highlight. For a family holiday letter, you can organize the letter so you separately discuss each member of the family, or you can write about the family in general. For a business holiday letter, you can call attention to the achievements the company made and goals for the coming year. Just be sure that this business information is safe to share with people outside of the company. Also be sure that you are writing a holiday letter and not giving an annual report, which is a separate document entirely. You may wish to thank your clients and colleagues for helping you achieve your goals and accomplishments. In both family and business holiday letters, extend your sentiments and wishes for your recipients to have a happy holiday season.

Third, your letter can be formal or casual in tone, and you could use the active or passive voice. Keep in mind, however, that you should have shorter, clearer sentences if you are using the active voice. Use the third person when referring to specific people if you want the letter to sound newslike. After all, the holiday letter is similar to a news bulletin or newsletter update. The format and design are not locked into any particular rules, but avoid using fonts that are too small or overly decorative, especially if you have a broad range of ages that will be reading it. What may be easy for you to read may not be for your 90-year-old grandfather. Even if you use images and other embellishments, keep the rest of the letter simple. Also consider what kind of information is appropriate to share and what is not. That is, if you have a naturally open and candid personality, some of your readers may not. Be sure to adjust your tone and language so your letter is safe to read aloud to the six-year-old in the family so you don't find yourself blushing at the next family reunion.

The New Year's Greeting

The New Year's holiday letter can be one way for both families and business owners to avoid the rush of the holiday season, gain some extra time to compose and send out their letters, and avoid the issue of offending anyone's religious or cultural preferences. While "Season's Greetings" is the generic holiday-card tagline, there are people who celebrate nothing at all, may celebrate more than one holiday, and some who take offense to "Happy Holidays" because they feel it fails to acknowledge the specific holiday they celebrate. There is very little question or chance for offense, however, with a New Year's greeting since most people in one fashion or another mark the New Year with January 1.

Family Holiday Letter

Season's Greetings from the Smith Family!

Well, we've had quite a year and thought that we'd take a moment to highlight some of the bright spots with all of you. Mark started teaching again, taking a position with the local university as an adjunct professor. He is excited about it but is amazed at how unprepared his freshmen students are sometimes. He also loves that his work hours give him more time at home with Jane, Doug, and Michael as well as time for his writing.

After years of troupe leading and organizing local events, Ellen changed her volunteer status with the Girl Scouts to take on a paid position within the organization. Ellen is ecstatic about the new adventure and about getting paid to do things she was already doing. Plus, with Mark home more often and Jane in college, she needed something to occupy her free time.

Jane has survived her first semester at Stanford and made the Dean's list. She hasn't yet settled on a major and chides her father for his commentary about unprepared freshmen. She's also playing intramural soccer, is on the debate team, and is glad to be home for winter break to see old friends and eat food that doesn't require a meal card.

Doug and Michael are doing fantastic as well. The twins are inseparable as ever. Both took up hockey this year and are proving to be quite the players. They, too, are excelling in school, both bringing home straight A's on their winter report cards. We have no idea how they manage to find time to hang out with their friends and play video games. Oh, that's right—most of their buddies also play hockey, and when they're not on the ice they're in our den feeding their faces and playing those video games. At least we know where they are!

It's nice to have the whole family home for winter break. The house is louder and a bit messier, but it is filled with laughter and joy—even Rusty our dog seems to be enjoying all the commotion and holiday craze.

We hope you, too, are finding the joy and delight of family and friends. We wish you all a happy, healthy, and prosperous new year filled with many, many blessings.

Love,

Mark, Ellen, Jane, Doug, Michael

Mark, Ellen, Jane, Doug, and Michael

Business Holiday Letter

Dear Colleagues and Friends:

As the holidays are a time to give thanks, we want to thank you, our clients and associates, for your business throughout the year. We would also like to take note of some of the highlights of 2007 that could not have been possible without your support, encouragement, and patronage.

We were recognized by the Chamber of Commerce as one of the top growing businesses in the area. We launched four new products, each to critical acclaim. Margaret Benson, head of finance and operations, received recognition as one of the leading business-women in our area. Matthew Platt and Geoff Laney became best-selling authors with their book on the industry, *The Story of Widgets: Industry Insiders Speak Out.* Overall, the company reached all of its benchmarks and was profitable in each quarter. As our gift to you, please use the link below to access your copy of *The Story of Widgets: Industry Insiders Speak Out.* You will also receive your very own signed copy of this best-selling book by mail to the address that we have for you on record.

We here at Laney, Laney, and Gherkin Widgets hope that you have a holiday season filled with cheer, delight, and blessings, and that you have a successful, prosperous, and happy new year.

Yours,

*Geoff Laney   Thomas Laney
Maria Gherkin*

Geoff Laney
Thomas Laney
Maria Gherkin

USEFUL WORDS AND PHRASES

Wishing you all the happy things
this very special holiday brings!

Tis the season to wrap the world in joy and love!

Wishing you a sleigh full of wishes
and dreams come true.

May your heart be filled with every joy
during this special time of year.

Wishing you and your family a
Christmas frosted with winter magic.

——————— USEFUL WORDS AND PHRASES (continued) ———————

Wishing you hot cocoa mornings and
fireside nights this Christmas.

Christmas is a special time of year, filled
with peace, love, and thankfulness.
Have a joyous season.

May the candles in your window spark
peace around the world. Happy Hanukkah!

May the blessings of Hanukkah brighten your life.

May the remembrance of the eight-day
miracle bless your family with hope and love.

May the Festival of Lights shine bright
with hope and happiness this Hanukkah season.

May the principles of Kwanzaa offer guidance
and comfort to you and your family.

Celebrate culture and community,
family and future! Happy Kwanzaa!

Let the countdown to a memorable
year begin! Happy New Year.

At this joyous time of year, keep friends
and family close at hand.

May God bless and keep you, now
and throughout the year.

Wishing you 365 chances to love, laugh,
and live your best year yet.

Tips

Do

- ✉ make the letter fun and engaging.

- ✉ use the passive or active voice and a casual or formal tone depending on your personal style.

- ✉ take into consideration the ages of your readers when writing your letter and using decorations or embellishments.

- ✉ show the personality of your family or business.

- ✉ highlight important achievements that were accomplished throughout the year.

- ✉ keep it upbeat and happy even if you're recognizing a solemn event such as the death of a loved one.

- ✉ match the envelopes with the stationery you use if you are sending your letter by regular mail.

- ✉ consider holiday mail times to ensure timely delivery, especially if sending holiday letters abroad.

- ✉ sign your letter.

Don't

- ✉ send the family holiday letter to business contacts unless they are close, personal friends.

- ✉ make the letter longer than one page. If you are using images and artwork, one sheet of legal-size paper is better than two sheets of letter-size paper.

- ✉ forget to wish your readers the appropriate holiday greeting.

- ✉ forget to place the recipient's addresses in the BCC (blind carbon copy) field or use a newsletter service (a company that will send your newsletter for you) if you are sending your letter electronically.

- ✉ get too personal in business holiday letters. Be sure to keep it professional.

CHAPTER
4

Business at Home

O UR OVERFLOWING MAILBOXES AT HOME are evidence that business letters don't just come to you at the office. Letters come to us daily regarding an array of issues—banking, credit cards, insurance, medical issues, solicitations, and more. Even though you're at home, the rules of business-writing etiquette still apply. After all, you are corresponding with a business, so your end of the conversation should be as professional as possible.

PERSONAL BUSINESS LETTERS

You don't need to be in business to know how to professionally present your written word. The skill of writing an efficient business letter (even if you are not a business professional yourself) is key in getting your needs met and your voice heard. Competent business writing may also increase the probability of a situation being handled effectively and quickly. Some appropriate situations for writing a business letter are when handling banking, lending, and investment issues, medical issues, insurance issues, tax issues, and dealing with contractors and service providers. Within this group, the appropriate scenarios for using a business letter include, but are not limited to, making requests for information or a particular service, making changes in service, updating personal information, reporting a complaint, and making a compliment.

When writing your personal business letters, use quality stationery and make sure your letter is typed out and not handwritten. This is when you should use the personal letterhead in your stationery wardrobe. Letters should be formatted in block or semi-block style and single spaced between lines and double spaced between paragraphs. Before writing your letter, make sure that you have the correct names and titles of anyone in the company who is relevant to the situation. Be sure to include key information such as account, reference, or invoice numbers. This makes it easier and faster for the company to access your file or account. However, never include your social security number, employer identification number, or tax identification number unless it is absolutely necessary. With the rise in identity theft, you do not want to give that information to potential thieves just in case your letter falls into the wrong hands.

An IRS Alphabet Soup: The Difference Between EINs, SSNs, and TINs

Employer Identification Number (EIN): Also known as a Federal Tax Identification Number, this is used to identify a business entity. Generally, businesses need an EIN.

Social Security Number (SSN): A personal identifier used by many U.S. entities. These include government agencies such as the Internal Revenue Service, as well as private agencies such as banks, health insurance companies, and employers. They have been adopted almost universally as the national identification number in the United States.

Taxpayer Identification Number (TIN): An identification number used by the Internal Revenue Service (IRS) in the administration of tax laws. It is issued either by the Social Security Administration (SSA) or the IRS.

The Paper Trail

If you're wondering why you should write a letter regarding a personal business situation instead of picking up the phone or sending an e-mail, it is because of the paper trail. Anyone who has seen popular court-related reality shows knows that without proper documentation, all you have is a series of "he said, she said," which will solve nothing, especially if it turns into a legal issue or ends up in litigation.

Documentation provides a chronological record of the events of the issue, which is important for you and whoever is involved in addressing the issue. Always make copies of your original signed letter. You can also scan it and save it to a disk. If you work in an office, do not use your company's business stationery for your personal business unless your company is acting on your behalf. In that case, there is probably a staff member who will handle the letter, so make sure that person has all the relevant information and that you receive copies of any letters written on your behalf.

How to Say It

When writing business letters, use the active voice. Be direct and firm but not caustic or aggressive. Be sure to address only the relevant information needed for handling the issue by using short, clear sentences. Your business letters should be no longer than two pages. In your closing, thank the recipient for their time and attention to the matter and include the best way they can contact you during business hours. If additional documentation is required, be sure to include that as well.

If a business matter relates to working directly with a person from the company, find out their supervisor's name so you can inform them of your experience. Be sure to briefly describe what the person helping you did and include all relevant dates of inter-action—especially if they were helping you with a matter over a long period of time. If you don't know the person's name, be extra detailed in sharing the times and dates of your interaction. Chances are the company has records of who worked when and will be able to match that with the information you provide.

The following examples show a variety of home-related business issues. The same writers are used for each letter to illustrate how many home business situations there are.

Financial Letter, including changes of name and address

Janet B. Lawson
514 Maplewood Circle
Appleton, WI 54913

October 25, 2008

Elizabeth Cormier
Account Manager
Big Investment and Annuity Firm
P.O. Box 0000
Chicago, IL 60611

Re: The Big Bank and Trust Company
    Annabelle J. Smyth
    Acct. No. ABC0000

Dear Ms. Cormier,

I am writing as a beneficiary of my grandmother's account and instructing you and The Big Bank and Trust Company to send the remaining shares assigned to me to my current address: 514 Maplewood Circle, Appleton, WI 54913.

Please note that at the time of the last disbursement of shares, as my grandmother's beneficiary, I was not yet married. It is likely that your records list me under my maiden name, Janet Elizabeth Bryce. It is also likely that the address of record is my address prior to my marriage:

5 Winchester Road, Evanston, IL 60202. I have included a copy of my marriage certificate to prove that the identities of Janet Elizabeth Bryce and Janet B. Lawson are one and the same. If you need any additional information, please do not hesitate to contact me at 920-555-2904.

Many thanks in advance for your assistance with this matter.

Very sincerely yours,

Janet B. Lawson

Janet B. Lawson
Beneficiary of Annabelle J. Smyth

Encl.

Protect Yourself—Guarding Against Identity Theft

When correspondence regarding business contains sensitive information such as SSNs or bank account numbers, pay close attention to the people or businesses that you are corresponding with. Do not freely give out your SSN, EIN, or TIN. If a company specifically asks for any of that information, do not hesitate to call them to verify. In most cases, if you are contacted by the Internal Revenue Service or a banking or lending institution, your identifying numbers will already appear on the correspondence. If you receive such information electronically and have never conducted business or requested to conduct business with that institution, do not complete the requested information. Don't be afraid to protect yourself and your identity. Never respond to an e-mail requesting that information.

Medical Insurance Letter

Janet B. Lawson
514 Maplewood Circle
Appleton, WI 54913

February 5, 2009

Big Medical Insurance Company (BMIC)
P.O. Box 1000
Milwaukee, WI 53201

Re: Group Number: 00000
    Contract Number: 123456789
    Policy Holder Name: Alan G. Lawson
    Patient Name: Samuel Bryce Lawson
    Issue: Billing for Well-baby Appointments

To Whom It May Concern:

We have received several bills from University Hospital Pediatrics regarding well-baby appointments and vaccinations for our son, Samuel Bryce Lawson. We have two medical insurance policies with BMIC through my company and my husband's company. After speaking with Marilyn G., a representative from BMIC, regarding our coverage, we learned that our first coverage with Major Accounting Firm, LLC, does not cover these appointments. However, our second coverage through the University of Wisconsin does.

We understand that when the first coverage is rejected, the issue should get bumped to the second coverage. In our case, it did not, as I learned when I spoke to Sandy B., a BMIC representative in the department that handles University polices. We were instructed to send the explanation of benefits letters (which are enclosed) so that the issue can be rectified, since our son's well-baby appointments and vaccinations should be covered by our plan with the University.

If you have any questions, please do not hesitate to call us at 920-555-2904. Thank you in advance for your expeditious assistance with this matter.

Yours sincerely,

Janet B. Lawson

Janet B. Lawson

Tax-related Financial Issue

Alan G. and Janet B. Lawson
514 Maplewood Circle
Appleton, WI 54913

September 27, 2008

Discovery and Tax Enforcement Division
P.O. Box 8949
Madison, WI 53708-8949

Re: Notice of Proposed Income Tax Adjustments for
   123-45-6789 and 987-65-4321

To Whom It May Concern,

We are writing to disagree with the adjustments made to our 2007 Wisconsin Tax Adjustment. We spoke with a Treasury Representative and were told of the documentation we needed to provide, part of which we did not receive from the originator until after the deadline. It was impossible to reply before September 17. We are responding now, at the first opportunity and immediately upon receiving the needed documentation for our rebuttal.

We disagree with the adjustments made to our 2008 Wisconsin Tax Adjustment for the following reasons:

1. The $134.00 proposed tax was already paid.

2. The wages earned, $3,356, for which those taxes were assessed, were not earned in the state of Wisconsin.

3. The wages earned, $3,356, for which those taxes were assessed, were not earned by a resident of the state of Wisconsin at the time.

4. The applicable taxes on those wages were paid to the state in which they were earned, Illinois.

Documentation and Reasoning:

The $3,356 (actual amount was $3,356.88) was earned during the month of January 2008, the only month Janet B. Lawson (then Janet Elizabeth Bryce) earned wages from Northwestern University in 2008. At the time, she was still a resident of Illinois, and she did not move to Wisconsin until February 1, 2008. She did not earn wages from Northwestern University after January 31, 2008.

The 2008 W-2 was missing because it was sent to the address-of-record with the Payroll Department at Northwestern University. (Copy of 2007 W2 from Northwestern University attached.) After speaking with the Payroll Department to obtain a copy of the 2008 W-2 form, it was determined that even though Janet Elizabeth Bryce had updated her address with other departments of the University, the W-2 went to her former (Illinois) address at the beginning of January 2009. By this time, any U.S. Postal Service forwarding orders to her new Wisconsin address had expired. The former address was 5 Winchester Road, Evanston, Illinois 60202. Furthermore, the wages were earned prior to her marriage to Alan G. Lawson in July 2007. (Copy of State of Wisconsin Certificate of Marriage and Marriage License are enclosed.)

Thus, according to the copies of the 2008 W-2 form as provided by Northwestern University, you will see that as a single wage earner at the time the wages were earned (by a resident of Illinois), $143.36 was paid to the state of Illinois. The correct state to which taxes were and should have been assessed is Illinois. We owe neither the proposed tax of $134.00 nor the interest of $30.00, for a total of $164.00, to the state of Wisconsin for the wages of $3,356. These wages were neither earned in Wisconsin nor by a resident of Wisconsin living as a nonresident in another state.

As per the instructions on the notice we received, a copy is also enclosed. Please correct our record. If you have any questions regarding this matter, please do not hesitate to contact us at 920-555-2904.

Many thanks for your time and assistance.

Respectfully yours,

Alan G. Lawson Janet B. Lawson

Alan G. Lawson and Janet B. Lawson

Encl.

Despite advice against doing so, the previous letter includes the social security numbers of the couple. In this case, it is acceptable because social security numbers, employer information numbers, and tax identification numbers are the equivalent of account numbers and how the Internal Revenue Service identifies people for tax-related matters. Additionally, the letter to which they were responding included their social security numbers, and the instructions stated to include those numbers on any correspondence regarding the matter.

Change of Service Letter

Alan G. Lawson
514 Maplewood Circle
Appleton, WI 54913

March 25, 2008

Big Medical Insurance Company (BMIC)
P.O. Box 1000
Milwaukee, WI 53201

ATTN: Ms. Frances Hansen, Policy Holder Customer Service Liaison

Re: Confirmation of service change for contract number 123456789

Dear Ms. Hansen:

Thank you for your assistance regarding adding my wife, Janet B. Lawson, to my policy. Though the human resources department at Big Major Accounting Firm did have the forms that I submitted for the significant-life-events benefits change, my wife is still not listed.

As per your instructions, below is the information and supporting documentation to ensure that the change is reflected in my account and its corresponding records.

✧ Group number: 012345

✧ Policyholder name: Alan G. Lawson

- ✧ Contract number: 123456789
- ✧ Added beneficiary: Janet Bryce Lawson
  Date of birth: June 5, 1968
- ✧ Effective date of change: March 10, 2008
- ✧ Copy of marriage license is enclosed as documentation.

Thank you for your continued assistance with this matter. If you need to reach me during business hours, please call me on my cell phone at 920-555-3332.

Yours sincerely,

Alan G. Lawson

Alan G. Lawson

HANDLING CONTRACTORS

When having work done on your house, such as adding an addition or making renovations, it may involve working with contractors and subcontractors no matter how big or small the project.

Although contracts with the company will be signed, it is still important to place any key communications with your contractor in writing—and that means a business letter. From the initial agreement through the final punch-list, putting requests, notifications, and changes in writing protects both you and the contractor you are working with. It also helps maintain a professional business relationship with the contractors no matter how friendly you may become during the course of the project.

Using the Lawsons as our example household, the following letters can be used in other general home-related business situations as well. They have also been written on the Lawsons' new personal business stationery, after they realized that with all the letters they write, they wanted to have their own letterhead.

Crossing Professional Barriers with Contractors and Other Workers in Your Home

No matter how friendly contractors or workers in your home may be and no matter how long they are in your employ, don't forget that they are providing a service. Becoming too friendly with those who work for you may result in more harm than good. It could make things difficult if you have a complaint because you may not want to seem pushy or mean to people who have become your friends.

The fact is that if you are paying them to do work, it should be done to your satisfaction and according to the agreed upon terms. This does not mean you have to be abrupt or aggressive, just remember to be careful not to let the lines of work-for-hire and friendship become blurred.

Confirmation of Services Letter

Alan G. and Janet B. Lawson
514 Maplewood Circle
Appleton, WI 54913

May 12, 2008

Paul Diamante, Owner
Additions and More
7360 Great Lakes Avenue
Appleton, WI 54913

Dear Paul:

It was a pleasure meeting with you and discussing the additional 255-square-foot room that will be built on the east end of the first floor of our house, as well as the necessary renovations to the existing infrastructure to bring all parts of the house up to present code. This includes changing our fuse box to a circuit breaker, updating the plumbing on the first floor to accommodate the half-bath that will be placed in the aforementioned room, proper insulation, and HVAC issues.

The new room will have a foundation built as well, and the renovation to the master bedroom will include a walk-in closet and connecting breezeway to the small bedroom adjacent to the master bedroom. The 255-square-foot room on the first floor will also have three skylights, built-in shelving units, and hardwood floors to match the hardwood that is throughout the existing structure. With all the renovations, you agree to use energy-efficient technology wherever possible.

Designs will follow the original concept that Alan and I created, modified per our meetings with you based on your building and construction expertise. We understand that work will commence on June 1. Prior to that date, we will make the necessary adjustments to our living space to accommodate when ground will be broken, walls knocked down, and the new and old structures united.

Payment for the project will be remitted as follows: one-third upon signing (done at our May 11 meeting); one-third halfway through the project; one-third at the end of the project. The final $350 will be paid upon completion of the project, which is determined after any issues on the punch-list have been resolved.

We are pleased that you and your team at Additions and More will be working on our renovation project, and we look forward to working with you over the coming months.

Very sincerely yours,

Janet B. Lawson

Janet B. Lawson

Change in Service Letter

Alan G. and Janet B. Lawson
514 Maplewood Circle
Appleton, WI 54913

July 26, 2008

Paul Diamante, Owner
Additions and More
7360 Great Lakes Avenue
Appleton, WI 54913

Re: Design change for walk-in closet

Dear Paul:

Thank you for the wonderful work that you have been doing. I want to confirm the changes that we discussed yesterday for the walk-in closet. Because of considerations about the style of the doors and how they open, they affect what will become the passage to the adjoining room, which will become a nursery. Instead of accordion folding doors for the closet, we would prefer the doors to be pocket doors. We realize that will entail restructuring the wall to be able to create the "pocket," and this will add both time and labor costs to the project. Please fax me the

projected increases and the new timetable to my home
fax number: 920-555-8955.

Sincerely yours,

Janet B. Lawson

Janet B. Lawson

The purpose of many letters dealing with contractors is to make
the entire process more simple and clear for both parties. The letters are straightforward ways of exchanging information. Complaint letters, on the other hand, present information on what
has happened *and* explain the reason why you are dissatisfied. As
with hate mail, if you are angry when composing your letter, be
sure to wait a day before looking at it again. Allowing yourself to
get all of your frustration out on paper can be therapeutic, but
sending an angry letter will not necessarily generate the kind of
response you seek. By waiting a day before sending the letter, you
will be able to read it with more objectivity and less emotion.
After you have slept on it for at least a day, edit and remove anything that could be interpreted as offensive or as a personal attack
on the recipient.

Though you may think that an angry letter will elicit a quick
response, it may only create more problems in the process. You
want to voice your frustration in a useful and tactful way that will
make the reader see that you mean business but are not a loose
cannon.

The Better Business Bureau and You

The Better Business Bureau (BBB) exists to provide consumers and businesses with an unbiased source to guide them
on matters of trust. Their services for consumers are free.
You can learn about businesses, report issues, and find other
public services. When in doubt about a company, check
with the BBB at www.bbb.com.

Complaint/Condemnation Letter

Alan G. and Janet B. Lawson
514 Maplewood Circle
Appleton, WI 54913

August 3, 2008

Paul Diamante, Owner
Additions and More
7360 Great Lakes Avenue
Appleton, WI 54913

Dear Paul:

Overall, we are pleased with the work you have been doing on the renovations and are looking forward to furnishing the addition downstairs. However, as I mentioned during our phone call, we have an issue with one of your subcontractors.

The group you sent to lay the parquet in the new room has not completed the job as anticipated or as Alan and I discussed with you. There are several issues that concern us. First, the threshold between the new room and the existing house is uneven and does not match the other thresholds on the level. Second, some areas are already buckling and need to be replaced. The bottom panel of one of the built-in units is marred and will need to be replaced.

We would like to have these issues rectified now rather than wait for them to be rectified when it comes time to do the punch-list. When asked when they were returning, John D. told me that they had finished the job. According to my assessment, they have not. Please have them return to take care of these unresolved issues as soon as possible. If you wish to discuss this further, I can be reached on my cell phone at 920–555–3443. I have enclosed photos of the areas mentioned.

Many thanks in advance for your prompt attention to this matter.

Sincerely yours,

Janet B. Lawson

Janet B. Lawson

Encl.

Unfortunately, most of us decide to pick up the pen when we are dissatisfied, want to file a complaint, or when responding to a letter initiated by a business. Complaints are the norm but commendations and praise are rare. However, you can change that with your business letters. Since customer satisfaction is one of the top priorities for companies, why not let them know when you are satisfied? It can go a long way to tell a company when you receive stellar service or a situation is handled effectively.

If the service relates to working directly with a person or group of people, find out who the person's supervisor is so that you can inform them of your positive experience. Be sure to briefly describe what the person helping you did. Also include relevant dates of interaction if they were helping you with a matter that was handled during an extended period. If you don't know the person's name, be as accurate as possible in sharing the times and dates of your interactions. Chances are highly likely that the company has records of who worked when and will be able to match them with the information you give. If you receive stellar service, go ahead and let the company know with a written letter.

Letter of Praise/Commendation Letter

Alan G. and Janet B. Lawson
514 Maplewood Circle
Appleton, WI 54913

September 4, 2008

Paul Diamante, Owner
Additions and More
7360 Great Lakes Avenue
Appleton, WI 54913

Dear Paul:

Thank you again for the excellent work you and your team at Additions and More did on our home renovations. We have received so many compliments from friends and family members about your work. Thank you for your honesty every step of the way and for addressing issues with the greatest sense of professionalism and consideration.

Mike and Larry were always on time, worked hard, and were respectful of our personal space. And with the exception of the one incident—which was rectified almost immediately—your subcontractors were equally professional and courteous.

Please know that we will be more than happy to refer you to anyone looking to make home improvement changes.

Very sincerely yours,

Janet B. Lawson

Janet B. Lawson

Tips

Do

- ✉ mail letters by regular mail or by fax. When sending them by fax, be sure to use a cover sheet and only send information that is not particularly sensitive or confidential, unless you are absolutely certain that only the person you are writing to will be handling your documents.

- ✉ use business letters when handling banking, lending and investment issues, medical issues, insurance issues, tax issues, dealing with contractors, and dealing with service providers.

- ✉ remember that responding to businesses with a letter can be more effective than a phone call.

- ✉ use high quality stationery.

- ✉ make sure your letter is typed and printed.

- ✉ make copies of your signed letter or get copies of letters written on your behalf.

- ✉ format the letter in block or semi-block format.

- ✉ format lines of a paragraph so they are single-spaced but separate paragraphs by two spaces.

- ✉ make sure that you have the names and titles of key people and the correct spellings of their names.

- ✉ include key information such as account numbers, reference numbers, or invoice numbers.

- ✉ let angry letters sit 24 hours before sending, then edit them until they are clear and objective.

- ✉ use the active voice.

- ✉ be direct and firm but not caustic or aggressive.
- ✉ address only the relevant information needed to have the issue handled by using short, clear sentences.
- ✉ explain the reason why you are dissatisfied in a complaint letter and present only the facts that led to your disappointment.
- ✉ voice your frustration but do so in a way that will be useful and tactful.
- ✉ thank the person for their time and attention to the matter.
- ✉ include the best way you can be reached during business hours.
- ✉ include relevant dates of previous interactions when communicating with a company.
- ✉ include copies of relevant supporting documents.
- ✉ allow for the time it takes for the mail to arrive and be processed if your letter warrants a response. Wait one to two weeks after you sent your letter to follow up with a phone call if you have not received a response. If you faxed your letter, wait three business days before making a follow-up call.

Don't
- ✉ use the letter to make personal attacks.
- ✉ send original documents, such as statements. Always keep original documentation and make copies for anything that needs to be mailed.
- ✉ make business letters longer than two pages.
- ✉ send your SSN, EIN, or TIN unless you are handling an issue with the IRS.

CHAPTER
5

Business at Work

WRITING BUSINESS LETTERS IS AMONG the tasks of many professionals. Writing a proper business letter is a crucial skill regardless of your place on the professional ladder. For those who have been writing business letters for what may seem like forever, you might find that things have changed. Although basic conventions and etiquette still apply, some of the rules have been updated and modernized. For those entering or reentering the business world, having these skills is an added value to your career, making you more of an asset—especially as you work your way up in the corporate world.

THE BUSINESS LETTER

You may be shocked to hear that many people, even educated college graduates, do not know how to write a simple business letter. Sadly, many general curriculum requirements do not include the basics of navigating an average day at an office, which includes writing a business letter or two.

When writing a business letter, use the active voice and short, clear sentences. Type and print the letter on company letterhead, or if you work from home and haven't invested in or designed your own letterhead, use good quality bond paper. Use block or semi-block format, and unless you are using letterhead, be sure to include your name, title, company, and address followed by the date on the next line. Next, insert the addressee's name, title, company, and address. The next line should start with "Dear" followed by the person's name and a colon, not a comma. If you are unfamiliar with the person to whom you are writing, use his or her title and surname. For example, if you are writing to Dr. Mark Rubenstein, but you do not know him well, use "Dear Dr. Rubenstein" instead of "Dear Mark." If you are unsure of the person's gender, use "Dear Leslie Goddard" instead of "Dear Mr. Goddard," since Leslie could be a woman.

These are critical professional courtesies. They can be the difference between a letter that gets read versus one that does not. If you are writing blindly (the written equivalent of a cold call, meaning the recipient is not expecting your letter), you can opt to use a more generic opening, such as the person's job title—especially if you do not have the name of a specific person. "Dear Branch Manager:", "Dear Editor:", or "To Whom It May Concern:" are all appropriate methods for addressing this issue.

Your opening paragraph and introductory sentence should be strong but not forceful. Let the person know why you are writing or what you are writing about.

In the following paragraphs, expand on your introduction and explain the information presented in the first paragraph, saving the last paragraph for a brief conclusion.

In the conclusion, thank the reader for their time and offer a way to contact you in response. You can also let the person know when you will be contacting them. Finally, end the letter with a complementary close, your typed name and title, and your signature.

With the exception of enclosures, keep letters to a two-page maximum. If enclosures are included, inform the reader in the body of the letter that additional material has been supplied and what it is.

There are many types of business correspondence you will encounter at work. All of these types of business correspondence should conform to the same basic standards and etiquette. Business etiquette always depends on the person you are addressing. Outside of e-mail, the most prevalent forms of business correspondence are:

- Facsimiles (faxes)
- Memoranda (memos)
- Cover Letters
- Résumés and Curriculum Vitaes (CVs)
- Follow-up Letters
- Thank-you Letters
- Contracts and Agreements
- Confirmation/Acknowledgment Letters
- Networking Letters

Other common forms of business correspondence include:

- Billing or Creditor Letters
- Sales or Pitch Letters
- Letters of Recommendation
- Termination or Involuntary Separation Letters
- Resignation or Voluntary Separation Letters

How frequently you use these letters will depend on what business you are in and will vary from company to company. However, the first group are types of business correspondence many professionals will encounter on a regular basis.

It is essential to get the reader's attention immediately, no matter what type of business you are writing about. A poorly formatted letter or one that does not get to the point quickly is bound to lose the recipient's interest. This sounds harsh, but everyone is pressed for time—especially business professionals—so you have to keep them engaged long enough to find out why your letter is important and why you stand out from the pack.

If you are already in business with the person you're writing to or have done business with them in the past, your letter should tell them why they should continue doing business with you or why they should do business with you again.

A badly written business letter is an instant turn off. Know that time is a precious commodity for everyone, so as a writer, you *should* take the time to make sure your correspondence cuts through the smoke and haze of mediocrity. After all, business professionals receive dozens of letters every week, so it is essential that your letter is one they want to read and one they want to follow up on. Let's start with the forms of businesss correspondence professionals encounter most frequently.

Facsimiles (Faxes)

The facsimile, often called telefax, telecopy, or simply fax, is a form of business communication that has been used for decades. With the prevalence of e-mail and online messaging, it does not hold the instant or nearly instant title it once did.

If you opt to fax the traditional way, your document should have a cover sheet. (Electronic fax, or e-fax, is discussed in chapter eight.) Like the heading of a written memo or e-mail, the cover sheet tells the reader when the fax was sent, to whom, from whom, for what, why, and what to do with the information. Most companies have preprinted fax cover sheets. This allows you to insert the relevant information by hand, which is acceptable. Avoid the temptation to use fax-cover sticky notes. They are convenient, but they don't afford you the same kind of document privacy that using a standard fax cover sheet does. They also do not look as professional as a letterhead cover sheet.

Setting Up Your Fax Correspondence

Your cover sheet should have the following basic format:

Fax Cover

Date:

To:

Telephone Number:

Fax Number:

From:

Telephone Number:

Fax Number:

Re:

Number of pages:

Body (optional)

Disclaimer (optional)

How to Write It

Fax Cover: While it may seem like a no-brainer, including "Fax Cover" on the cover sheet alerts the person on the receiving end that this particular fax is separate from any other faxes that might have come before or after it. Alternatively, you can include your company logo or letterhead to further distinguish your faxes.

Date: Insert the date you are sending the fax.

To: This is where you put the name and title of the person you are faxing. This ensures that the recipient receives it, especially if there is one central machine for all incoming faxes.

Telephone Number: This is where you put the recipient's telephone number, including the extension, if applicable. Another apparent no-brainer, this allows the addressee to be contacted and alerted that they have a fax, especially if there is one central fax machine for all incoming faxes.

Fax Number: This is where you put the recipient's fax number. Also, it puts the number right at your fingertips—very convenient for you as you dial.

From: This is where your name and title are placed. This informs the person who you are.

Telephone Number: This is where your telephone number is placed so that either the recipient can contact you directly or the actual person receiving the fax can contact you if you accidentally dialed the wrong number.

Fax Number: This is where your fax number is placed so that the recipient knows how to reach you via fax. Even though it is required by telecommunications law for a fax machine to imprint transmission data on the fax, it's not always easy to read. Including your fax number and the other pertinent information makes it easy for the recipient to quickly contact you.

Re: This is where you put a brief summary of the subject of the fax.

Number of pages: This lets the recipient and addressee (if they are not the same person) know how many pages the fax is. Variations on this include "Number of pages including cover sheet," "Total number of pages," and "Number of pages after cover sheet."

Body: This is where you can include a brief note on the cover sheet itself. If you choose to include a message to the recipient on the cover sheet, keep it brief. A sentence as short as "Here are your requested materials" is sufficient.

Disclaimer: Another optional part of the fax cover sheet is a running footer with a statement about privacy and confidentiality. Include information about who to contact and how to do so in case the document has been received by the wrong person. A privacy or confidentiality statement is included in the following example.

Fax Cover Sheet

Fax Cover
Date: September 12, 2008
To: Doug Williams
Telephone Number: 313-555-9007
Fax Number: 313-555-9023

From: Marie Frances, Conference Coordinator
Telephone Number: 617-555-2751
Fax Number: 617-555-2701

Re: Conference Accommodations

Number of pages following fax cover: 4

Doug:

It was a pleasure speaking with you. Here are the documents you requested regarding the conference itinerary. Please call me if you have any questions.

Marie

This transmittal is confidential and for the intended recipients only. If you have received it in error, please contact Marla Meyers at Big Deal Conferences at 617-555-2790.

Be careful when sending a fax to someone who has not requested contact via fax or when sending advertisements or business pitches. Doing so is the fax equivalent of spam, and fax numbers are included in the guidelines for the Federal Do Not Call list. Violating the Federal Do Not Call list has stiff penalties, so it's wise not to send blind faxes.

Tips

Do

- ☒ include the date.
- ☒ include the fax and telephone numbers of the person you are faxing.
- ☒ include your fax and telephone numbers.
- ☒ indicate the number of pages of the fax.
- ☒ use a cover sheet.
- ☒ include a way to contact you should the fax be sent to the wrong person.
- ☒ keep any additional text on your cover sheet brief.

Don't

- ☒ send blind faxes.
- ☒ use fax cover sticky notes.

Memoranda (Memos)

Memos follow a similar format to faxes. In many ways, the format of the fax cover sheet is an evolution of the memorandum. Memos are usually short, one page long, and are sent to a group of people. They may accompany other documents and serve as an introduction to those documents. Memo format is as follows:

Memo (or Memorandum)

Date:

To:

From:

Re:

How to Write It

Faxes and memos do not need to be signed, although some people opt to place their initials by their name as a shorthanded signature. The reasons for each field are the same as those outlined for faxes. You can use the active or passive voice for memos. Memos should be brief and to the point, similar to the body of fax cover sheets. They can also be formal or informal depending on the subject or content. They should also be written on letterhead, typed, and printed. Remember to note whether punctuation is used. If a colon does not follow the field title (such as "Date," "To," or "From"), put the field titles in a bold font.

Memo

Memo

Date: June 1, 2008
To: Accounting Department
From: George Memowriter, CEO

Re: Summer Shutdown

This is a reminder that we will be closed during the first two weeks of July (July 1 through 15) for Summer Shutdown. Summer Shutdown is to balance the vacation blackout period during the increased hours and workload over the first two weeks of April in preparation for tax season. Please mark your calendars.

If you are already approved for vacation days during the Summer Shutdown period, please be sure to coordinate with Human Resources to adjust your schedule so that you do not lose your vacation time.

Any questions can be directed to Julia McIntyre.

GM

Cover Letters

The cover letter is often the first encounter a business professional will have with you, and sometimes it is the only chance you get at a positive first impression. Usually aligned with job seeking, cover letters are your way of introducing yourself or are the initial presentation of the materials you are sending.

Cover letters should be concise and no longer than one page. They should state the objective or purpose of the correspondence and briefly make a pitch about what you are offering, whether it is yourself as a job candidate, materials for a project, or other documents. You do not want to reiterate everything in your package or proposal in your cover letter, but you want to give the salient highlights about the main and most impressive points of the package or proposal. As with any business correspondence, print your cover letter on quality bond paper and use matching envelopes.

How to Say It

Format your letter in block or semi-block format, starting with your name and address if you aren't using letterhead, the date, and the addressee's name and address. Use quality stationery, letterhead, or your personal business stationery and make sure your letter is typed. The letter should be single-spaced except between paragraphs, which should be separated by one line. Before writing your letter, make sure that you have the correct spelling and titles of the person or people you are addressing.

The style of your cover letter may vary from situation to situation or from business to business, but overall it should conform to these basic principles. It is best to use the active voice, which is more direct and allows you to write shorter, succinct sentences. Open the letter by introducing the purpose for writing, such as applying for a job. End the letter by thanking the reader for their time, state how you can be contacted, and end with a complementary close before your signature.

Cover Letter for Job Seeker

James Sampson
57 Appleton Street
Jackson, MS 39201

May 15, 2008

Mr. Lloyd J. Manning, CEO
Thinktank Associates
5005 Industrial Way
Jackson, MS 39204

Dear Mr. Manning:

As a ten-year veteran of research and development at Major Worldwide Company, I am applying for the position listed in the recent issue of *Research & Development*.

While Thinktank Associates is a relatively new company, I am interested in bringing my expertise from MWC to help Thinktank grow. I have worked on key projects that increased the profile and net profits of MWC by 20 percent during my tenure. As a potential candidate for Thinktank, I believe my skills will help make the company become a major player in the R&D field.

My current résumé is enclosed as well as a list of references. I can be reached on my cell at 601-555-2598. I look forward to hearing from you and thank you in advance for your time and attention.

Yours sincerely,

James Sampson

James Sampson

Encl.

General Cover Letter Response

Mr. Lloyd J. Manning, CEO
Thinktank Associates
5005 Industrial Way
Jackson, MS 39204

July 15, 2008

Mr. James Sampson
57 Appleton Street
Jackson, MS 39201

Dear James:

It was a pleasure meeting with you last week. I wanted to write to you personally because not only was I impressed by your qualifications after meeting you, I was also certain I had to get you on board. I would like to offer you the position of Director of Research and Development.

Enclosed are materials from our human resources department, including our employment agreement, requisite tax forms, and full job description. I hope you will accept the position. Please let me know the earliest date you would be able to start, and from there we can set an appointment with our office manager, Ms. Higgins, to take care of arrangements for your orientation to the company.

I look forward to hearing from you soon.

Yours sincerely,

Lloyd J. Manning

Lloyd J. Manning, CEO
Thinktank Associates

Encl.

——— USEFUL WORDS AND PHRASES ———

Thank you in advance for your time.

I appreciate your consideration.

It was a pleasure meeting you.

Per your instructions, I am sending you ___.

I am writing to inform you ___.

I am writing you to apply for the position as ___.

I am writing you to apply for the position
listed in [publication or Web site].

I can be reached at ___.

I look forward to hearing from you.

I look forward to speaking with you.

Please let me know if this is of interest.

I would like to arrange a suitable time
for us to meet and discuss ___.

This letter is to confirm ___.

It was a pleasure meeting you on [day] at [location].

Based on our conversation, I believe I [or you]
am [are] a fantastic fit for this position.

Tips

Do

- ✉ use company letterhead or personal stationery on good quality bond paper.
- ✉ keep letters to a two-page maximum.
- ✉ type and print your business letters.
- ✉ use block or semi-block format.
- ✉ always sign your letters.
- ✉ make sure you correctly spell the name of the person you are writing to.
- ✉ make sure you have the correct job title of the person you are writing to.
- ✉ always proofread your letters before sending them.
- ✉ use the active voice.
- ✉ use short, clear sentences.
- ✉ engage your reader in the opening paragraph.
- ✉ tell or remind the reader why you are writing.
- ✉ thank the reader for their time.
- ✉ include how the reader can contact you or how and when you will contact them.

Don't

- ✉ use the person's first name unless you are already familiar with them or if they have already invited you to call them by their first name.
- ✉ assume the person you are writing to is male. If unsure, use their job title or first and last names.
- ✉ open your letter with "Dear Sirs" or "Gentlemen" unless you know with absolute certainty that you are writing to a group of men.
- ✉ ramble on. State your point quickly and succinctly.

Résumés and Curriculum Vitaes (CVs)

In 1975, one of the characters in *A Chorus Line* sang, "Who am I anyway? Am I my résumé? A portrait of a person I don't know?" In so many ways, this is true. Your résumé or curriculum vitae is your profile—your professional portrait—that gives the reader information about you, your experience, skills, and qualifications. It is your first impression and will help the person reading your résumé determine whether they want to learn more about you in an interview.

Though résumé and curriculum vitae (CV) are terms often used interchangeably, there are several differences between the résumé and the CV. First among them is length. Résumés should be no longer than two pages, whereas CVs can be four to five pages. The CV tends to be used overseas for jobs more than in the United States, where it is mainly used for academic, medical, research, and related fields, including writing and publishing. The résumé is a highlighted summary of one's work experience. A CV is a full dossier of all work experience, including jobs and positions held, research, publications, skills, and languages. For American candidates applying for jobs overseas, visa status is also indicated on the CV. It may also include personal data such as your date of birth and overall health. When including personal information, never include your social security number unless it is required to apply for the job.

How to Write It

Both résumés and CVs should include your full contact information, education, and work experience with dates for each. Bullets can be used to separate the key points in each section. However, the elements of a CV tend to be written in paragraph form. For every section, be as accurate as possible. Start with the most recent experience and work in reverse chronological order. With the exception of the first entry on job descriptions—which is your current or most recent job, internship, or relevant experience—statements should be in the past tense.

Your full name should be on each sheet of your résumé. They should be printed on white, cream, or ecru paper. Occasionally, light grey is acceptable, but avoid any other odd or "fun" colors. The goal is to keep the document as clean, professional, and streamlined as possible. These documents should also be easy to read, so avoid using multiple fonts or ones that are fancy or difficult to read. Use a simple font such as Times New Roman, Courier, or Arial. Book Antiqua and Palatino are also acceptable substitutes. The font should be between 10 points and 12 points. Use bold and italics sparingly. It is okay to bold or use all upper-case for headings, but don't use both. Alternatively, it is okay to italicize or bold a heading, but again, don't use both. Make sure that there is enough separation between sections, called white space, so it's easier to read. The margins should be one inch around, with the exception of the margin between the header and the top of the page, which should be no less than half an inch.

When it comes to design—even if you're applying for a position in one of the creative fields—résumés and CVs should not be creative. These are serious documents that, for many employers, initiate the weeding process.

When citing publications in CVs, use the appropriate bibliographic format and style for your field:

- MLA format for general humanities
- APA format for psychology
- Chicago or AP for writing and publishing

If you are unsure which style your field uses, look at a professional journal for your field and use their citation style as an example.

Provide at least three references for your résumé or CV on a separate sheet of paper. Your list of references should include each person's name, title, affiliation, address, telephone number, and e-mail address, along with their preferred way to be contacted. Don't forget to ask the people on your reference list if they are willing to be a reference for you. Do not include family members or a reference you're unsure will give you a stellar recommendation. If you do not wish to include a list of references with your résumé or CV, simply state at the bottom of the page that references are available upon request.

There are three main categories of résumés: novice, functional, and executive. The novice résumé is for those first entering the job market and are usually students or recent graduates. Functional résumés are used for those with gaps in their employment history or who are reentering the job market after a considerable hiatus. Executive résumés are for those with several years of job experience and leadership positions. Sometimes résumés are used to update an employee's file because they have changed positions within a company or have had a significant career event, such as an award, patent, or major publication.

Outline of the Basic Résumé

Full name and contact information: This information can be used as a running header. Make sure to include your home and cell phone numbers and your personal e-mail address. If you are already employed, do not include your work e-mail address.

Objective: Specifically state the purpose of the résumé customized for the position you seek. In the case of résumés used to update a file, this field can be omitted.

Education: In reverse chronological order from highest degree attained to high school, list the school name, the city, state, and country in which it's located (if applicable), degree earned, and field of study. You can either include the dates of attendance or only the graduation year. If you are an older adult, you may leave you date of graduation off your résumé to avoid giving your approximate age.

Experience: List your job history in reverse chronological order. Include the company name, the city, state, and country in which it's located (if applicable), your job title, and dates of employment. Follow that data with your job responsibilities and achievements.

Skills: List any relevant skills for the position sought. This may include languages you are proficient in and at what level. For example, you could be fluent in Spanish or only conversational in the language. You could also include computer software programs in which you are experienced.

For functional and executive résumés, the education field can be moved to the end so the reader sees your work experience first. Moving the education field to this position can also be helpful if you have a lot of work experience but may be unsure if your education level would be a hindrance to your application. In this case, you are not lying or being dishonest—you are still providing the information, just highlighting your professional qualities and experience by presenting them first.

Outline of the Curriculum Vitae

A curriculum vitae will follow the outline of a resume, but it will also include these factors:

Publications and Research Experience: List any published materials you have written or coauthored in reverse chronological order. Also include work that is pending publication. That is, work that has been accepted by a publisher or journal but may not have been printed yet. Use the full bibliographic format that is appropriate for your field along with a brief abstract of the publication.

Awards and Honors: This should include any awards that you have received in reverse chronological order, including the name of the award, what it was for and why, and the date received.

Professional Affiliations: Any guilds, associations, or organizations that you belong to that directly relate to your career.

Personal Information: This section would contain your visa status if applying for a job outside your native country, date of birth, and any other personal information that is desired for the position sought.

Novice Résumé

James Sampson
57 Appleton Street
Jackson, MS 39201
601-555-2598
jsampson@professional.com

OBJECTIVE

To obtain a leadership position with a growing company where I can use my research skills to improve the company's position within the chemical engineering industry.

EDUCATION

M.En. Industrial Engineering   **1991**
University of Southern California   Los Angeles, CA

B.S.Ch.En   **1988**
summa cum laude
Massachusetts Institute of Technology   Cambridge, MA
Participant in the ChE National Undergraduate
AIChE Contest

EXPERIENCE

Industrial Coatings Engineer   **Feb. 1991–Mar. 1993**
Plastics Labs   Jackson, MS

✧ Performed compliance regulation tests primarily for
   the industrial coatings division.

✧ Researched existing and new models for coatings including plastics, polymers, urethanes, and their application primarily for the industrial coatings division.

✧ Wrote standard reports.

Industrial Coatings Research **Jun. 1989–Feb. 1991**
Plastics Labs   Jackson, MS

✧ Worked closely with senior Industrial Coatings Engineer in research and development on grant proposals.

✧ Assisted with research for developing polymers with better adhesion properties.

✧ Assisted with research for developing improved safety features and regulations in conjunction with the senior Industrial Coatings Engineer.

Petrochemicals Intern/Fellow **May 1988–Apr. 1989**
GiantChem Labs   Cambridge, MA

✧ Worked closely with senior petrochemicals engineer on various research projects.

References available upon request.

Functional Résumé

James Sampson
57 Appleton Street
Jackson, MS 39201
601-555-2598
jsampson@professional.com

PROFILE/PROFESSIONAL SUMMARY.
Seventeen-year veteran of high-level research and development projects in industrial coatings for major worldwide companies. Experienced with older and current models, including VOC compliance, as well as writing industry-related articles about the employment of new technologies in industrial coatings and related fields.

EXPERIENCE

Senior R&D Engineer   **Jun. 1998–Present**
The Other Big Thinktank   Jackson, MS
5 Industrial Way, Suite 100

◇ Use engineering, physics, and chemistry backgrounds for research and development of new industrial coatings.

◇ Develop improvements to existing models for industrial coatings.

◇ Write detailed compliance reports.

◇ Write grant proposals.

◇ Train and supervise junior-level R&D engineers.

◇ Work in conjunction with company director on establishing green and earth-friendly codes for the company.

◇ Write articles for industry journals and trade magazines.

Project Leader   **Feb. 1993–Jun. 1998**
Uberbig Industrial Labs   Jackson, MS
Industrial Coatings Division

◇ Oversaw research and development of industrial coatings division projects.

◇ Met with regulators to ensure compliance with industrial coatings standards.

◇ Provided detailed reports to senior level management and board of directors.

◇ Wrote articles for industry journals and trade magazines. (Samples and full citation list available upon request.)

Industrial Engineer—R&D   **Feb. 1991–Mar. 1993**
Medium Labs   Jackson, MS

◇ Performed compliance regulation tests primarily for the industrial coatings division.

◇ Researched existing and new models for coatings including plastics, polymers, urethanes, and their application primarily for the industrial coatings division.

◇ Wrote standard reports.

EDUCATION

M.S. Industrial Engineering   **1991**
University of Southern California   Los Angeles, CA

B.S.Ch.En   **1988**
Massachusetts Institute of Technology   Cambridge, MA

PROFESSIONAL MEMBERSHIPS/HONORS

Chartered Chemical Engineer
Member, American Institute of Chemical Engineers
Member, Association for Process Safety Research
Member, Institute for Sustainability

ADDITIONAL SKILLS

Fluent in French and German

References available upon request.

Electronic Resources for Job Seekers

The days of searching through the newspaper for a job are over! The Internet has many fantastic resources for job seekers, including

www.careerbuilder.com	www.quintcareers.com
www.hotjobs.com	www.resumes.com
www.jobseeking.com	www.salary.com
www.monster.com	www.seekingsuccess.com

─────── **USEFUL WORDS AND PHRASES** ───────

Responsibilities included ___.

Responsible for overseeing ___

Assisted with ___.

Directed ___.

Established ___.

Developed ___.

Secured placements in [publications]
regarding ___.

Provided assistance for ___ on a daily basis.

Led team in [project].

Contributed to ___.

Projects included ___.

Achieved record sales for [product].

Gained valuable experience working with ___.

Special skills include [typing speed,
strong organizational skills, etc.].

Fluent [or conversational]
in [language].

Tips

Do

- ✉ be as specific as possible regarding dates and responsibilities.

- ✉ list jobs and positions you have held in reverse chronological order.

- ✉ write in the past tense with the exception of your currently held position.

- ✉ write in the active voice.

- ✉ have your résumé or CV proofread by someone else.

- ✉ use bold and italic sparingly.

- ✉ use a simple, legible font.

- ✉ make sure your résumé is no longer than two pages.

Don't

- ✉ undersell yourself. Don't be afaid to showcase your accomplishments.

- ✉ exaggerate your past experience.

- ✉ use the word "resume," which means "to begin again." Be sure to use the accents over both letters "e."

- ✉ forget to include your contact information, including your home and cell phone numbers and your e-mail address.

- ✉ use the e-mail account of your current job to send your résumé to potential employers. Use your personal e-mail if you don't want your current employer to know that you're applying for a new job.

- ✉ include your social security number.

- ✉ include references who will give a negative assessment of you.

- ✉ print your résumé on colorful paper. Use white, cream, ecru, or light grey.

Follow-up Letters

Follow-up letters should be used to inquire whether previous correspondence has been received or when following up on arrangements. In this case they are considered confirmation letters, acknowledgement letters, or acceptance letters.

When writing a follow-up letter that also acts as a confirmation letter or letter of acceptance, use letterhead or quality bond paper and type the letter. In certain cases, using e-mail is also appropriate, but it should still follow the format of a written letter.

Letters of acceptance should match the formality of the invitation or arrangements. Format the letter with your address (unless using letterhead), followed by the date and the addressee's address. Using the active voice, be brief and sincere; do not write more than one page. Thank the reader for the invitation, and be specific about the invitation or arrangement details. Tell the reader that you are looking forward to the event or whatever it is that you are accepting. End with a complementary close followed by your name and signature.

When using follow-up letters to inquire if an earlier correspondence has been received, be sure to allow enough time to pass between the initial correspondence and your follow-up letter. Three to four weeks is a good waiting period, as it will allow time for the mail to arrive, the letter to go through the internal channels of reaching the recipient, and for the recipient to address your letter.

Pay close attention to the company policies when writing follow-up letters. Some companies specifically state their average time frame for responding to letters. Some company policies state up front not to send a follow-up. Ignoring these guidelines does not show that you have tenacity, it shows that you cannot follow directions or that you did not read the policies. Either way, it is an easy way to have your initial correspondence not addressed at all.

Using block or semi-block format, write your follow-up letter on company letterhead. Use the active voice. Be direct but not forceful, and give the reader the benefit of the doubt, as opposed to writing with an accusing tone. For all you know, they were on vacation or out sick when you sent the initial letter. Restate the reason for your initial correspondence, and inform the reader that this letter is a follow-up letter. Also include the date of your initial correspondence and briefly state the details of the situation for which you are following up.

Do not make demands that the recipient respond, but give them a possible time frame for when you can be reached and your contact information. Alternatively, tell them when you will touch base with them. End the letter by thanking them again for their time followed by a complementary close and your signature.

———— USEFUL WORDS AND PHRASES ————

I am following up with you regarding ___.

I would like to touch base on ___.

This letter is to confirm our arrangements
regarding ___.

I initially wrote to you regarding ___.

I look forward to hearing from you.

I wanted to ensure that you received my materials.

Please do not hesitate to contact me
at [e-mail address or phone number].

I am available most afternoons after [time].

Tips ————————————————————

Do

- ✉ include a brief summary of the original correspondence.
- ✉ include details about what you are following up on.
- ✉ be sincere.
- ✉ use the active voice.
- ✉ give the reader the benefit of the doubt.
- ✉ make sure you are aware of the recipient's policy on time frame for responses.
- ✉ suggest a time when you are available to speak with or when you will call the recipient.
- ✉ use clear, simple sentences.
- ✉ keep your follow-up letter to one page.

Don't

- ✉ be forceful or overbearing.
- ✉ be demanding.
- ✉ be rude or intimidating.

Professional Thank-You Letters

Thank-you notes should always be sent from a candidate to a prospective employer after a job interview, when someone has assisted you, and even to employees and colleagues in appreciation for and recognition of a job well done.

Go back to chapter two, which covers how to format professional thank-you notes. Professional thank-you notes should be short, have the active voice, and be written in standard business format on company letterhead.

Contracts and Agreements

Both contracts and agreements are similar in that they show that two or more parties are in agreement about an offer and the terms of that offer, and also that they have willingly entered the agreement. Some contracts are binding, meaning the law will recognize them. Should a breach of contract occur, the law will uphold the contract and determine the consequences if the contract is broken.

Legally binding contracts and agreements should be drafted by an attorney so that they conform to the specific format unique to binding contracts and that they contain all appropriate elements. If you are choosing to use a binding contract, work with an attorney. However, non-binding contracts are not considered legal documents. These are often called letters of agreement.

How to Write It

Letters of agreement state who is entering the agreement, what the agreement is for, the length of time that the agreement covers (for example, "two years" or "through project completion"), and whether there are any consequences for either party violating the terms of the agreement. There is often language in the letter of agreement that states that one or both of the parties are entering the agreement voluntarily.

When writing a letter of agreement, use letterhead and block or semi-block format. Write in the active voice and use short, clear sentences and plain language. Since this kind of contract is non-binding, there is no need to try to imitate legal prose in a letter of agreement. Simply make the document as clear and easy to understand as possible for both parties. Begin by giving a brief summary of what you are both agreeing to. This might be only one or two sentences. Next, list each term of the agreement. Describe the terms in detail. To make each point or term of the agreement even more clear, you can offset each by numerical bullet points. Be sure to include specific dates and times where necessary if the contract calls for it.

Letter of Agreement

Jules Madison
Madison Associates
7230 Magnolia Boulevard
Santa Barbara, CA 93101

November 30, 2008

Anthony Zwieback
Chandler Group
5600 West Road
Santa Barbara, CA 93101

Dear Anthony:

Thank you for inviting me to speak at the "Moving Forward" symposium in February. I am more than happy to speak at the symposium for the agreed-upon speaker's honorarium of $300.00. I just want to confirm that the symposium is scheduled for Wednesday, February 11 through Friday, February 13, 2009, at the Hyatt Regency. My presentation on building your business identity will be about 30 minutes long, with additional time for a question-and-answer period with audience members. I look forward to receiving more details from you about the event particulars. Please let me know which type of audio visual or multimedia equipment will be available.

I eagerly await hearing from you and being part of this year's Moving Forward symposium.

Yours sincerely,

Jules Madison

Jules Madison
Madison Associates

—————— USEFUL WORDS AND PHRASES ——————

As per our agreement

I am writing regarding our arrangements about ___.

It is my understanding that your
responsibilities shall include ___.

Comply

Please respond if I have forgotten anything.

Tips

Do

- ✉ be specific about the terms of the agreement.
- ✉ countersign the agreement after it has been signed and returned to you.
- ✉ provide copies of the agreement to all parties involved.
- ✉ have an attorney draft it, if choosing to use a binding contract.
- ✉ use the active voice (except where legal language is used).
- ✉ write in short, clear, easily understood sentences.
- ✉ divide each portion of the contract or letter of agreement into sections for more clarity if necessary.

Don't

- ✉ make threats in the contract.
- ✉ use legal-sounding language in a letter of agreement when you are not an attorney writing the contract.

OTHER COMMON BUSINESS CORRESPONDENCE

Some of the others types of business correspondence that one might encounter on a regular basis are billing and creditor letters, sales letters, letters of recommendation, termination or involuntary separation letters, and resignation letters.

Billing and Creditor Letters

Billing letters should be direct and written in the active voice. Unless you are using a special billing program, billing software, or a form for your invoice, they should be written on letterhead and in block or semi-block format. Use short, clear sentences and include the amount due, the service or product the invoice or bill is for, and the date payment is due. Include information regarding how you will accept payment and if there are any surcharges or fees for late payments or returned checks. Instruct the customer or client whether their account number or invoice number should also appear on their check if they pay by check. Be sure to include a way for the client or customer to contact you if they have questions about their bill or need to dispute any charges on their bill as well as the address where payment should be sent—especially if it is a different address than the company's main street address.

Payment Reminders

Sometimes payment will not have been received and you will need to send another notice. When this occurs, make sure you have allowed sufficient time for the bill to be received, filed, and payment sent. Once you have determined that payment has not been sent by the time frame indicated on the original bill, send a second notice.

How to Write It

Using letterhead and block or semi-block format, your letter can be more cordial than the original billing letter. However, give the payer the benefit of the doubt rather than taking an accusing tone. Suggest that perhaps they forgot or that the payment and second notice have "crossed in the mail." Restate the original charges including any late fees that may have been assessed, referring to the late-fee surcharge policy of your company.

Be direct and use the active voice with clear, short sentences. As with the initial invoice, describe ways payment can be sent, when payment is due (which in this case is usually "upon receipt"), and further penalties for non-payment. Include the date of the original bill and a way for you to be contacted to discuss any issues pertaining to the invoice.

If payment has not been remitted after you send the second notice, you may need to send a final notice. The final notice is the last step a company takes before transferring the job of collecting payment to a third party. Be firm and direct. State the original charges, any new late fees that have been assessed, and the company policy for late or unpaid bills. Provide contact information to discuss the invoice or to settle a dispute. Inform the customer or client what the next steps will be should the bill continue to go unpaid.

First Invoice Billing Letter

Juno Web Design
3568 Longwharf Avenue
Boston, MA 02110

June 2, 2008

Ms. Shura Bandele
57 Commonwealth Avenue
Boston, MA 02116

Re: Invoice, Account No. 59873

Dear Ms. Bandele:

Thank you for choosing Juno Web Design for your project. Per our agreement, this is the invoice for the Web design project completed for you on May 20, 2008. As per our initial agreement, the fee for 20 hours of design—which included writing your copy, designing your logo, ensuring SEO (search engine optimization), and creating a shopping cart and user forms for your ten-page Web site—is $1,350. We have recorded your initial deposit of $450, one-third of the estimated final fee. Please pay the remaining $900 within 21 business days by check or money order. Please note that a $33 fee will be imposed on returned checks. Payments not received within 21 days will incur a late fee of 1.5% per day.

If you wish to make a payment electronically by direct transfer from your bank account or with a credit card, contact our billing office at 617-555-6003. Otherwise, please include your account number on your check or money order and send it to:

Juno Web Design
Billing
P.O. Box 9008
Boston, MA 02116-9872

If you have any questions about your bill, please do not hesitate to contact us. Thank you again for your business, and we hope you will continue to choose Juno Web Design for your future Web design needs.

Sincerely yours,

Marcus Sandberg
Marcus Sandberg
Juno Web Design

Second Notice

Juno Web Design
3568 Longwharf Avenue
Boston, MA 02110

July 1, 2008

Ms. Shura Bandele
57 Commonwealth Avenue
Boston, MA 02116

Re: Invoice—Second Notice, Account No. 59873

Dear Ms. Bandele:

Thank you again for choosing Juno Web Design. Unfortunately, we have not received payment for the Web design project completed on May 20, 2008. We provided 20 hours of design—which included writing your copy, designing your logo, ensuring SEO (search engine optimization), and creating a shopping cart and user forms for your ten-page Web site—for a total cost of $1,350. The initial invoice for the balance owed of $900 was sent on June 1, 2008. Payment was due within 21 business days of the invoice date, and as of today, your balance will be charged an additional 1.5% per day. The new amount due as of this date is $1,230.35 and is due upon receipt. If payment has been sent, disregard this notice. Otherwise, please remit payment upon receipt of this notice with a check or money order.

If you wish to make a payment electronically by direct transfer from your bank account or with a credit card or need to discuss your invoice, contact our billing office at 617-555-6003. When paying, include your account number on your check or money order and send it to:

Juno Web Design
Billing
P.O. Box 9008
Boston, MA 02116–9872

Thank you again for your business, and we hope you will continue to choose Juno Web Design for your future Web design needs.

Sincerely yours,

Marcus Sandberg

Marcus Sandberg
Juno Web Design

Final Notice

Juno Web Design
3568 Longwharf Avenue
Boston, MA 02110

August 1, 2008

Ms. Shura Bandele
57 Commonwealth Avenue
Boston, MA 02116

Re: Invoice—Final Notice, Account No. 59873

Dear Ms. Bandele:

Unfortunately, after two attempts to collect payment for the Web design project completed on May 20, 2008, your account with us is still unsettled. We provided 20 hours of design—which included writing your copy, designing your logo, ensuring SEO (search engine optimization), and creating a shopping cart and user forms for your ten-page Web site—for a total cost of $1,350. The initial invoice for the remaining balance owed of $900 was sent on June 1, 2008. Payment was due within 21 business days of the invoice date, and as of June 30, your balance has been charged an additional 1.5 % per day. The new amount due as of this date is $1,732.79 and is due upon receipt.

Contact our billing office at 617-555-6003 as soon as possible to discuss your account and to arrange payment options. If we have not heard from you within 21 days of receipt of this notice, we will be forced to send your account to a third party for collection.

We look forward to hearing from you soon to take care of this matter.

Sincerely yours,

Marcus Sandberg

Marcus Sandberg
Juno Web Design

———— **USEFUL WORDS AND PHRASES** ————

Invoice/bill

Remit

Due within __ days.

Due within __ business days
(specify number of business days)

Past due

Total amount due upon receipt: ___

Surcharges

Fees

I am writing to inform you regarding ___.

Prompt payment is appreciated.

Tips ————————————————————————————

Do

- ✉ be clear and direct on the invoice.
- ✉ state all of the charges on the invoice.
- ✉ give a due date.
- ✉ explain penalties for returned checks and late payments.
- ✉ give a way to contact you if there is a question or dispute about charges.
- ✉ keep the invoice to one page.

Don't

- ✉ be forceful or intimidating on a first attempt to collect payment.

Sales Letters

Sales letters can be annoying. When people get them, they know they are being offered some product or service they probably don't want want or need. These letters clog our mailboxes because the companies who write sales letters have purchased our names from marketing lists based on other purchases we have made in the past.

The unsolicited sales letter is a nuisance, but as a professional, you can successfully use sales letters and pitches with existing clients or with people who have expressed an interest in your product or service and are already on your company mailing list.

How to Write It

Open your letter with a personal touch and a good "hook." Without sounding like a used car salesperson, explain in the first sentence what the product or service is. Then describe it and explain why your product or service is important and different from any others like it, perhaps providing relevant statistics to your target market. Follow by telling them how they can learn more, or if they are ready, how to purchase and a way to respond to your advertisement. Thank the reader for their time, and follow with a complementary close.

The format can be memo, simple letter, or standard block or semi-block. Depending on the product and your relationship with the client, choose an informal or formal tone but write in the active voice.

Sales Letter

Widget Company
9501 Widget Lane
Louisville, KY 40201

Dear Widget Company Valued Customer:

Super Ultra Widgets are the new product we will begin offering this fall. Thirty percent stronger than our patented Super Widgets and 50 percent stronger than our standard Original Widgets, they will make your life easier and workday smoother.

Become more efficient and streamlined with Super Ultra Widgets! You already know about the value, performance, and tested reliability of Original Widgets and Super Widgets, so why not try our new Super Ultra Widgets before they are released to the public?

For a limited time, we are offering Super Ultra Widgets at up to 20 percent discount. We want to give you every advantage in trying the new, improved Super Ultra Widgets. Just for trying Super Ultra Widgets, you will get

10 percent off of your order. If you are unsatisfied for any reason, you have our usual unconditional money-back guarantee. Refer a colleague or friend to Widget Company, and if they join our client family, you get an additional 10 percent off your existing order.

You know that Widget Company stands for value, integrity, and service, so please try our newest addition to the Widget Company product line—Super Ultra Widgets. Contact us at 800-555-5555 for more information or to opt out of our service offers. You may also visit our Web site at www.widgetco.com/suwpromo and enter your customer number to take advantage of this special limited time offer.

Thank you for your time and attention and for your continued faith in Widget Company

Sincerely,

Burt Leherer

Burt Leherer
President of Marketing and Sales
Widget Company

────────── **USEFUL WORDS AND PHRASES** ──────────

A great value

___ will help cut costs at your establishment.

We promise high quality.

This offer is good at no additional cost.

Research shows that ___.

Statistics show ___.

I would be happy to offer a free sample/trial offer before you decide.

No obligation

This promotional offer is valid through [date].

We offer ___ at your convenience.

Risk-free

Exclusive offer

Are you in need of ___ at this time?

Are you looking for ___?

We would like to share this opportunity with you.

Thank you for your time and attention.

Refer a colleague or friend for an additional special offer.

Tips

Do

☒ be sincere.

☒ be direct about the product or service.

☒ describe the product or service in clear, simple terms.

☒ give the reader a way to respond.

☒ use the active voice.

☒ cross reference with your company's internal "no solici-tations" list if you are using a purchased marketing list.

Don't

☒ be forceful.

☒ make the letter longer than one page.

☒ send the letter to people who have requested not to receive such information from you.

☒ forget to give your potential client a way to contact you to purchase *and* a way to contact you to opt out.

Professional Letters of Recommenation

During the course of your professional life, you may be asked to write letters of recommendation. Letters of recommendation should be short and sincere and should only discuss relevant qualities of the person you are recommending. Leadership skills, organizational skills, ability to problem solve, and the person's ability to interact with customers, colleagues, or the public are things to consider writing about in the letter.

How to Write It

A professional letter of recommendation should be written on personal letterhead unless you are writing as a representative of a company, in which case it should be written on company letterhead. Do not be afraid to give short but specific, concrete examples. State why you are recommending the person and what the recommendation is for. This lets the reader know that you are aware of the circumstances for the letter of recommendation and allows you to further tailor your letter to that situation. At the end of the letter, thank the reader for their time and offer the best way you can be contacted if they wish to speak to you directly. Finally, use the complementary close followed by your signature and title.

Letter of Recommendation

Sam Alicea
675 Lakeshore Drive
Chicago, IL 60611

August 5, 2008

Mr. Lloyd J. Manning, CEO
Thinktank Associates
5005 Industrial Way
Jackson, MS 39204

Re: Letter of Recommendation for James Sampson

Dear Mr. Manning:

I understand that James Sampson has applied for a position with Thinktank Associates. James and I worked together for seven years on several projects with The Other Big Thinktank. I retired from the company three years ago. Throughout my relationship with James, I cannot say that I have met or worked with a finer person. His tenacity and problem-solving skills are phenomenal, and he has a gift for thinking "outside the box" in order to maximize the potential for R&D projects. As I am sure you already know, he has several publications under his belt, and as such, has proven strong research skills and an ability to communicate them well to his colleagues both in writing and in person.

I highly recommend James for the position of Director of Research and Development at Thinktank Associates. I have watched him blossom in his career, and the time is ripe for him to take on new challenges and have the chance to truly put his leadership skills to good use.

If you have any questions or wish to speak with me directly about James, I am more than happy to do so. Please do not hesitate to call. I can be reached at 724-555-9784 anytime.

Very sincerely yours,

Sam Alicea

Sam Alicea

--------- **USEFUL WORDS AND PHRASES** ---------

[Candidate's name]'s experience as [position] has given her [or him] the skills to succeed at your company.

I highly recommend [candidate's name] for this position at [company's name].

Due to his [or her] leadership skills and proven work ethic, [candidate's name] will be an asset to your company.

His [or her] responsibilities included __.

After __ years, [candidate's name] has successfully achieved ___.

Tips

Do

- ✉ be honest and sincere—speak from your heart but use professional language.
- ✉ use the active voice.
- ✉ speak about the candidate's relevant best qualities.
- ✉ only discuss the candidate professionally.
- ✉ offer a way to be contacted for further discussion.

Don't

- ✉ mention anything that would put the candidate in a negative light.
- ✉ make your letter more than two pages.
- ✉ exaggerate the candidate's experience or skills.

Termination and Involuntary Separation Letters

Termination letters are an unfortunate necessity in business. Often called "pink slips," they can be singular or group letters. The latter scenario should only be used when there is a department or company-wide separation or layoff. They are called involuntary separations because the employee receiving one has not decided on their own to leave the company.

How to Write It

Any termination or separation letter should be honest, candid, sincere, and written in the active voice. It is best to use block or semi-block format, and it should be written on company letter-head. State the reasons for the termination or involuntary separation and when it becomes effective. When warranted, include language about other terms of the separation such as severance pay, gag orders, or agreements not to sue the company.

When sending a singular termination letter, be candid but do not use the letter to attack the employee's personal traits. Only discuss the termination as it relates to their job or job performance. When writing about the reasons for a singular termination, include any references to previous probationary periods or chances given to the employee to rectify behavior that was against company policy. Group termination letters can be in block, semi-block, simple, or memo format. Singular termination letters should be in block or semi-block format and directly addressed to the employee.

Group Termination Letter

Company Letterhead
Beechwood-Purcell Associates

Memorandum

To: All employees

From: Matthew Sutherland, CEO
Beechwood-Purcell Associates

Date: April 10, 2008

Re: Company Cutbacks and Layoffs

Dear Valued Employees:

As you all know, our quarterly earnings have been well below the projected forecasts for more than a year. As such, we have made many cuts in order to keep the company afloat, including cutting the salaries of directors and those in upper management and only giving cost-of-living raises rather than merit increases. Even with such measures, we have yet to achieve positive earnings. Because of this situation, we regret that during the coming months we will be making cutbacks among the staff across all departments. This is not an easy decision, and it will be an even harder decision as supervisors will be instrumental in identifying the areas where cuts need to be made.

Employees who are identified for involuntary separation will be given severance pay commensurate with experience and length of service with the company, COBRA information for continued out-of-pocket health insurance among other benefits to be fully determined by the company Board, Corporate Counsel, and Human Resources. The final date of attachment with the company will be two weeks from the date the individual involuntary separation letters are sent.

We sincerely regret having to take these measures, and in advance we thank all of our employees for their service. We wish those who will be selected for involuntary separation the best in all of their future endeavors.

Sincerely yours,

Matthew Sutherland

Matthew Sutherland, CEO
Beechwood-Purcell Associates

Individual Termination Letter

Mr. Lloyd J. Manning, CEO
Thinktank Associates
5005 Industrial Way
Jackson, MS 39204

February 20, 2008

Ms. Louisa Simpson
971 River Road
Jackson, MS 39201

Dear Ms. Simpson:

We regret to inform you that after several poor reports and evaluations from your immediate supervisor along with the continued infractions of company policy with respect to personal calls, conducting personal business at work, inappropriate dress, tardiness, and customer complaints, we are terminating your employment. Even with being placed on probation through the appropriate human resources channels, improvement has not occurred in any of these instances. You are advised to clear the office of your personal property, transfer any work for the company to your supervisor, and turn in your keys to human resources within three business days.

We sincerely regret that this is the decision we have been forced to make and wish you better success with your next employer.

Sincerely yours,

Lloyd J. Manning
Lloyd J. Manning, CEO

─────── **USEFUL WORDS AND PHRASES** ───────

We sincerely regret to
inform you that ___.

We are no longer able to accommodate you
as an employee of [company name].

We wish you the best of luck in
your future endeavors.

We are certain you will rise from
this difficult setback.

Please be sure to [clean out your office,
turn in your key] by [time and date].

We regret to inform you that due to
[reasons], we are terminating your
employment at [company name].

Because improvements have not been
made, we feel that we have no choice
but to terminate your employment.

Based on your previous evaluation,
we must terminate your employment.

We regret that this is the decision
we have come to.

If you have any questions or there is
anything else you would like to discuss,
please see me [or Human Resources].

Tips

Do

- ☒ be direct, honest, and sincere.
- ☒ include effective dates.
- ☒ include information about separation provisions.
- ☒ provide necessary forms for separation where applicable.
- ☒ make sure the termination is legal ahead of time.
- ☒ include specific reasons for termination.
- ☒ offer to meet with the employee regarding any questions or concerns they may have.

Don't

- ☒ use a singular termination letter as a forum to make personal attacks.

Resignation and Voluntary Separation Letters

Resignation letters or voluntary separation letters are used to inform your employer that you are leaving the company. The standard time frame to give notice is two weeks, but it can be longer, especially when the separation is amicable. You may need to (or want to) train or otherwise assist your replacement or finish projects that you have begun before you leave the company. Before resigning, double-check company policy for how and when they need to be notified, and you should always officially notify the company in writing.

How to Write It

Write your letter on personal stationery or personal letterhead in block or semi-block format. Start with the purpose of your letter and include something positive about your experience with the company. You want to leave on good terms and don't want to burn any bridges, especially if there is the possibility that you may ask someone from the company to write a letter of recommendation or to be a professional reference for you in the future. In your letter, state why you are leaving the company as well as the date of your last day. Where relevant, provide information for how unfinished projects may be resolved or to whom you will be handing those projects prior to your last day. Close the letter by thanking the company and provide your new contact information and how you can be reached after your last day. End your letter with a complementary close and your signature.

Resignation Letter

James Sampson
57 Appleton Street
Jackson, MS 39201

October 1, 2008

Mike Matheson
The Other Big Thinktank
7009 Main Street
Jackson, MS 39204

Dear Mr. Matheson:

After more than a decade with The Other Big Thinktank, it is time for me to broaden my horizons. As you know, Thinktank Associates has been courting me for some time. I am writing you to announce that I have accepted a position with Thinktank Associates to be their Director of Research and Development.

I have enjoyed working with you and my colleagues and interns here at The Other Big Thinktank. I have enjoyed contributing to this company, but I am sure you will understand my desire for more responsibility as my chief reason for leaving.

My last day here will be October 31, 2008, and in the interim, I will begin handing projects over to Ms. Samms, whom I understand has been selected as my replacement in the event that I accepted the position at Thinktank Associates.

I hope we will continue to stay in touch. As of November 15, my new work address will be Thinktank Associates, 5005 Industrial Way, Jackson, MS 39204. My telephone number will be 601-555-9701. My personal address and telephone numbers will not change. At the very least, I hope to see you at next year's Thinktank Conference in Houston.

With warmest regards and many thanks.

Sincerely yours,

James Sampson

James Sampson

USEFUL WORDS AND PHRASES

I have truly enjoyed working with you.

I cannot thank you enough for
the valuable experience.

My experience here has been very positive.

My last day will be [date].

Thank you for the opportunity.

My work at [company] was
extremely rewarding.

I wish [company name] all the best.

I hope we will continue to stay in touch.

Please let me know if there is anything else
I can do to help with this transition.

Tips

Do

- ✉ give a minimum of two weeks notice.
- ✉ be sure to mention that you appreciate the experience you have gained while working for their company.
- ✉ assure them you will complete any unfinished projects before your last day.
- ✉ use personal letterhead or personal business stationery.
- ✉ make a copy of the letter for yourself.
- ✉ give them your personal information so they can contact you after you leave.

Don't

- ✉ use the resignation letter as a forum to tell the company about their negative aspects.
- ✉ use company letterhead for your resignation.

CHAPTER
6

School-related and Extracurricular Correspondence

I T CAN BE DIFFICULT FOR parents to decipher when it's appropriate to correspond with teachers, coaches, and school administrators. Many parents want to give their children a certain level of independence and teach them responsibility, but it's important to know ways you should be involved with academic and school-related correspondence and when it should be your child's responsibility.

We'll discuss academic writing as well as writing in relation to educational activities and extracurricular groups, clubs, organizations, and teams. This chapter will cover all levels of education from elementary through secondary school, post-secondary school, and similarly structured programs. It involves introduction letters, short notes regarding absences, questions directed to teachers, and year-end thank-you notes, as well as navigating an academic application package.

LETTERS FROM PARENTS TO TEACHERS

Establishing communication between parents and teachers is essential for ensuring that a student's needs are met. E-mail is not always effective because not everyone checks it often. Telephone calls are not optimal either for a number of reasons; unless a teacher has given parents his or her personal contact information, the best time to call is probably during school hours, which is also when she or he is teaching. Phone calls from teachers can sometimes yield unpleasant responses from parents caught off guard, and from there communication can go downhill. Short letters and notes between parents and teachers, however, can be effective. Because of the popularity of e-mail and the convenience of picking up the phone, they may not receive many letters from parents. Teachers or adminstrators will appreciate that you took the time to write.

Inquiries About Goals and Expectations

There are a variety of reasons for parents to write to teachers and administrators. When fostering a community of learning that actively involves the teacher-parent-student triad, letters and short notes can pave the way for open and respectful communication. Don't just rely on flyers, school billboards, school Web sites, or your child for announcements and pertinent information.

How to Write It

Using personal stationery or letterhead, set this letter in block or semi-block format and write in the active voice. The tone can be formal or informal, but it should not seem too casual even if an informal tone is used. You want to show the school and teacher that you are interested in understanding their goals and expectations in a respectful way.

Goals and Expectations Inquiry

Robert and Elizabeth Petersen
291 Drake Circle
Bellinghamton, WI 53562

September 7, 2008

Ms. Julia Lardie
Bellinghamton Senior High School
351 Lincoln Road
Bellinghamton, WI 53562

Dear Ms. Lardie,

We are concerned about the courses that our daughter, Sarah-Beth, is taking this year. It seems that none of the classes on her freshman schedule are college-preparatory classes. We know that she tested well and had excellent grades throughout elementary and middle schools, so I am sure that you can understand our concern that the classes on her schedule are not going to prepare her adequately for college work.

We hope to schedule a meeting with you in person to discuss Sarah-Beth's schedule and the goals and expectations for her as a freshman. We would like to arrange a meeting as soon as possible so she does not fall behind in the more advanced classes.

I can be reached at 606-555-9781. Thank you for your time and attention, and I look forward to hearing from you soon.

Sincerely yours,

Robert Petersen

Robert Petersen

Notes Regarding Behavior and Grades

Waiting until there is a severe problem regarding your child's behavior or grades is too late; instead it is a good idea for parents to contact teachers and administrators about brewing issues by mail when the issue is first brought to your attention. The letter should be more of an alert to the teacher or administrator that there seems to be an issue and that you would like to discuss it. Avoid making assumptions about the teacher or administrator's awareness of the situation before speaking with him or her— especially if it is a situation that involves another student. Stress that your concern is to meet your child's best interests and how you as a parent can work to meet those expectations with the teachers and administration.

How to Write It

Using personal stationery or letterhead, set the letter in block or semi-block format. Use the active voice and a formal, but not forceful, tone. Since this is for such an important matter, type the letter instead of handwriting it. Start the letter by informing the instructor or administrator of the problem. Express the reasons for your concern and request a meeting with the teacher or administrator (or both) to discuss the issue in person. Include the best way to contact you so that the meeting can be arranged. End with a complementary close and your signature.

Letter About Behavior
or Grades

Robert and Elizabeth Petersen
291 Drake Circle
Bellinghamton, WI 53562

December 1, 2008

Mr. Malcolm Roberts
Bellinghamton Senior High School
351 Lincoln Road
Bellinghamton, WI 53562

Dear Mr. Roberts,

Thank you for your note. My wife and I agree that the sophomore year of high school is a very important year, and that Josh's midsemester report card was quite disappointing. His grades are clearly below where they should be. We are also concerned about what you described as his "frequent disruptions."

We agree that Josh has great potential and is not meeting it, and we would like to set up a meeting with you to discuss this. I work from home and can meet with you during the day. We can also set up an evening appointment if you wish to meet with Elizabeth and me. Perhaps early next week would be a good time since it will be right before the winter break, which we might be able to use to our advantage.

Our home phone number is 606-555-9781. We look forward to hearing from you soon.

Yours sincerely,

Robert Petersen

Robert Petersen

cc: Andrew Murray, Principal

Remember that Teachers Are People, Too

When writing to teachers and other instructors—especially when it comes to complaints—keep in mind that whatever the situation, you may have only heard part of the story.

When you write to them, be firm but be polite and not overly aggressive. Write the letter from the point of view that you and the teacher want your child to succeed. If you are not getting the results you and your child need or envision, however, you always have the option to meet with the teacher's superiors.

Letter About Behavior or Grades

Robert and Elizabeth Petersen
291 Drake Circle
Bellinghamton, WI 53562

November 4, 2008

Dr. Elayne Stockington
William H. Lincoln School
1025 Jefferson Street
Bellinghamton, WI 53562

Dear Dr. Stockington,

Our youngest child, Chad, is a sixth grader in Mr. Pendleton's homeroom. Chad has brought to our attention that some eighth graders have been continually harassing sixth-grade students.

Through informal discussions with other parents after hearing our children talk, it seems that this has become a regular occurrence. We have taught Chad to avoid bullies and not to engage with them. However, it seems that each week this group of eighth graders seeks out some sixth grader to harass, and then these sixth graders get in trouble when they are trying to defend themselves. What's worse is that the eighth graders seem to escape punishment completely.

The most recent episode resulted in Chad receiving a detention after punching one of the bullies, as we are sure you know. We don't condone his use of violence, but it seems he was at the breaking point and saw no other solution. We wish to discuss this grave situation with you and Mr. Pendleton as soon as possible, and we would like to set up a meeting in person.

We can be reached at 606-555-9781. Thank you in advance for a timely response.

Respectfully yours,

Robert Petersen Elizabeth Petersen

Robert and Elizabeth Petersen

Concerns and Complaints

No teacher or administrator likes to receive angry letters. Unfortunately, sometimes they do. It is important for parents and guardians to remember that there is a person on the other end of that letter. We need to be especially careful when writing a complaint letter to a teacher or school staff member because it's difficult to *not* be emotional when it comes to our kids.

Letters are better than phone calls or e-mails in these situations because writing the letter gives you a chance to get your anger out before sending it. Stating the same thing on the phone or clicking "send" on a hastily composed, fiery e-mail can lead to regrettable consequences.

How to Write It

On personal stationery or other quality paper, draft your letter to the appropriate faculty or staff member, and use block or semi-block format. Handwriting your letter is acceptable, but it's wise to type such an important letter. Use the active voice and choose the formal or informal tone depending on your personal preference. Be sure to address only the relevant information needed to discuss the issue and use short, clear sentences. Explain why you are dissatisfied, and present the facts that led to your disappointment. State your concern or reasons for wanting to meet in person to discuss the issue.

Don't be accusing or make personal attacks on a teacher or staff member. If you are angry when composing your letter, be sure to wait a day before looking at it again. Sending an angry letter will not generate the response you seek. By waiting a day before sending the letter, you will be able to look at it with more objectivity. After you have let the note or letter sit, edit it and remove anything that could be interpreted as a personal attack on the recipient. Inform the teacher of your availability and provide your contact information and the best time and way to reach you. End with a complementary close and signature.

Complaint

Geoffrey Sullivan
727 Oxford Road
Bellinghamton, WI 53562

December 5, 2008

Mr. Albert Payne
William H. Lincoln School
1025 Jefferson Street
Bellinghamton, WI 53562

Dear Mr. Payne,

I would like to schedule a meeting with you to discuss Sarah's homework. I find it odd that she never seems to have any. Sarah says she completes it before school ends—sometimes before class ends—because it is so easy. I am a little concerned that she may not be challenged enough, and I'm wondering what we should be doing at home. I work from home and can be reached there on most days.

If you are available after school on Wednesdays, I can meet with you then. My number is 606-555-9712. I look forward to hearing from you soon.

Sincerely,

Geoff Sullivan

Geoff Sullivan

Notice how this letter was very simple and straight to the point even though he was communicating a complaint to his daughter's teacher. Keeping things professional as opposed to emotional and angry in a letter will make a teacher or administrator more willing to discuss such concerns with a parent.

─────── USEFUL WORDS AND PHRASES ───────

I look forward to hearing from you.

We are concerned about ___.

I do not believe [student] is reaching his [or her]
full potential in preparation for college.

I would like to arrange a meeting with you
on [date] at [time] at [location].

I look forward to speaking with you soon.

academic enrichment

We'd like you ensure that ___.

I'd like to discuss what I can do to be more
involved in his [or her] schoolwork.

curriculum standards

I can be reached at ___.

Are you available to meet regarding ___?

Thank you for your time and attention.

I hope we can work together to ___.

I'd like to bring to your attention that ___.

I appreciate a timely response.

I would like to take this opportunity
to inform you about ___.

I am writing this letter to remind you that ___.

My child's best interests

Frequent disruptions [or tardiness, absence]

We believe ___ is a pressing matter.

We wish to discuss this matter
in person as soon as possible.

Your involvement is the key to resolving
this grave issue.

We are disappointed about ___.

We would like to discuss your suggestions
regarding this matter.

Tips

Do

- ✉ be sincere and show your genuine interest in resolving the problem.
- ✉ use personal stationery or letterhead.
- ✉ use the active voice.
- ✉ use the formal or informal tone, depending on the circumstance.
- ✉ spell out consequences, results, or resolutions you wish to see.
- ✉ provide documentation where necessary, such as a report card or detention slip.
- ✉ suggest when you are available and provide contact information.
- ✉ mention the purpose of the letter and what you hope to accomplish by writing it.
- ✉ copy the principal and other senior administrators or school administrative assistants if you don't feel that your concerns are being properly addressed.
- ✉ clearly state what you wish to accomplish with the letter, whether that is to schedule a meeting or to get information from the teacher or staff member.
- ✉ address the teacher or administrator with respect and courtesy.
- ✉ sign the letter.
- ✉ keep a copy of the letter for your records.

Don't

- ✉ be forceful.
- ✉ be too informal or casual.
- ✉ be unprofessional.
- ✉ handwrite a letter of importance.

LETTERS FROM
STUDENTS TO TEACHERS

Sometimes a student might want to write to their teacher or instructor for various reasons, including wanting to thank them for something, scheduling a meeting to discuss a grade, or wishing to start a club or organization. Writing a letter to your teacher is a personal touch that will show them you are serious about your grades and education. If you are in school and under 18, inform your parents so that they are aware of the situation—this will protect you and the teacher.

How to Write It

On personal stationery or other good paper, draft your letter to the appropriate faculty or staff member and use block or semi-block format. You can handwrite or type the letter. Use the active voice and choose the formal or informal tone depending on your personal preference. Be sure to state the specific reason for writing the letter. Inform the teacher of your availability and suggest when you are free during school hours, offer to see them during their office hours, or briefly after school. End with a complementary close, and be sure to sign the letter.

Teacher Appreciation Around the World

Across the world, countries celebrate teachers and the contributions they make to children everywhere. From Tunisia to Sweden to Honduras and everywhere in between, people are sharing their appreciation for teachers and all they do, whether they are their own teachers, their former teachers, or their children's teachers. There is also a World Teacher's Day every year on October 5. United States National Teacher Day and Teacher Week are celebrated in schools across the country. Traditionally, National Teacher Day is the Tuesday of the first full week in May, and that entire week is considered Teacher Appreciation Week.

Letter from a Student to a Teacher

Geoff Sullivan, Jr.
727 Oxford Road
Bellinghamton, WI 53562

December 13, 2008

Mr. Malcolm Roberts
Bellinghamton Senior High School
351 Lincoln Road
Bellinghamton, WI 53562

Dear Mr. Roberts,

Thank you for your help with the sources for my history paper. I'd also like to meet with you about a couple of things. First, I'm interested in taking the AP history class next semester and wanted to know what you would recommend for me. Second, a few of us have been thinking about starting a history club and wanted to know if you'd be our faculty advisor. I have fourth period free on Tuesdays and Thursdays, and I'm usually free on Fridays immediately after school. I hope that you'll be available to talk soon, especially since I would like to finalize my second-semester schedule before winter break. I'll touch base with you after our next class.

Sincerely,

Geoff Sullivan, Jr.

Geoff Sullivan, Jr.

─────── **USEFUL WORDS AND PHRASES** ───────

I cannot thank you enough for
counseling me on choosing a college.
You really helped make my decision easier!

I would like to discuss ___.

I would like to schedule a time
for us to meet regarding ___.

I hope you are available
to go over ___.

An apple just isn't enough to show how
much I appreciate your help!

I appreciate the comments you made on my
project, and I would like to meet with you
in person to discuss them in further detail.

A few of us are thinking about starting
a [club or organization], and we would like to know
if you would be our faculty advisor.

I would not have succeeded in this class
without you as my teacher. Thank you.

Tips

Do

- ✉ use the active voice.
- ✉ suggest a possible time to meet that works with the teacher's schedule.
- ✉ tell the teacher directly if there is an action that you need from them.
- ✉ use the semi-block format for your typed or handwritten letter.
- ✉ be polite and respectful.
- ✉ make sure your parents are aware that you are writing the letter.

Don't

- ✉ make the letter longer than one page.
- ✉ forget to sign your letter.

NOTES FOR OUTINGS AND FIELD TRIPS ORGANIZED BY PARENT VOLUNTEERS

Advanced planning is crucial when alerting parents and guardians about possible outings and field trips. Like with any other invitation to an event, parents and guardians should be given enough time to respond and decide if their child can or should participate, and they need all the information about the proposed outing.

How to Write It

Include information about possible cost, lunch arrangements, location, times and scheduling, method of transportation, the purpose of the outing, and how it relates to the curriculum or extracurricular activity. Also include a permission slip and a due date for its return with the parent or guardian's signature and any fees that should be collected in advance. If the trip or activity is a relatively expensive one, be sure to include information about any financial support that might be available for families and the deadlines for applying.

Using school letterhead, set in block, semi-block, or memo format. Use the active voice. Describe the trip or activity using a formal or informal tone.

Field Trip Letter

William H. Lincoln School
1025 Jefferson Street
Bellinghamton, WI 53562

February 10, 2009

Dear Fourth Grade Parents and Guardians,

As part of the Social Studies unit on Government, we are helping Mrs. Pat Serbinsky and Ms. Ellen Baer plan the annual fourth grade trip to the state house in Madison. Students will get a tour of the state house and have the opportunity to meet and speak to Representative Alan Swenson, our district representative. This is a trip that the fourth grade does every year, and we are grateful to Rep. Swenson for making time in his schedule to meet with us again.

The trip is planned for Friday, March 20, 2009. Students should arrive at school on time and report to homeroom where attendance will be taken. From there, the classes will assemble in the auditorium for a head count and announcements at 8:20 A.M. We expect to start boarding the buses at 9:00 A.M., and we plan to leave the school at 9:15 A.M. We expect to arrive at the state house at 10:00 A.M. We will return to the school at 3:15 P.M. Students should dress warmly and bring their lunch and an afternoon snack with them, along with a notebook and pens or pencils.

Please note, because of post–9/11 security, everyone will need to go through the security checkpoint and all bags will be examined. It is also imperative that you return the permission slip by the deadline, as we need to provide security at the state house with a list of the names of every child and adult participating in the trip beforehand. The trip schedule and permission slip are enclosed. Please sign and return the enclosed permission slip no later than March 1, 2009.

If there are any parents who wish to chaperone, please call Mrs. Danbury, field trip coordinator, at the school office at 606-555-2300, ext. 15.

Sincerely,

Jane Bernstein   Georgia Sollars

Jane Bernstein and Georgia Sollars
Fourth Grade Parent Volunteers

Encl: permission slip, itinerary

CC: Mrs. Pat Serbinsky and Ms. Ellen Baer
　　　Fourth Grade Teachers, William H. Lincoln School

—————— USEFUL WORDS AND PHRASES ——————

planning

weather permitting

Please sign and return the
permission slip by [date].

Permissions slips and schedules are enclosed.

If you are interested in chaperoning
the field trip, please contact ___.

Tips ————————————————————————

Do

- ✉ include how the trip relates to the curriculum.
- ✉ include all pertinent information.
- ✉ include the name of a contact person and their phone number.
- ✉ provide the complete, detailed itinerary.
- ✉ use the active voice.
- ✉ use school letterhead.
- ✉ invite other parents to be chaperones, if possible.

Don't

- ✉ forget the permission slip or any other necessary enclosures.

NOTES FROM PARENTS TO
ORGANIZATIONS AND ADMINISTRATORS

Most schools and school systems have a variety of parent-led organizations from Band Boosters to the Parent Teacher Associations (PTA) or Parent Teacher Organization (PTO). If you would like to begin an organization or have an idea that will benefit the school as a whole, the parent-teacher group or the adminstration are the ones to contact directly.

Starting an Organization

When trying to establish an organization at your school, first do background research well in advance of approaching the school with the idea. After you have done the necessary research, contact the school administration to see what the correct channels are for starting a club or organization. Present a sound plan for the organization or group, including its function and purpose, duties, projected expectations from the school in terms of participation and support (whether financial or otherwise), and expectations from members. Make sure that you have provisions in place for fund-raising, bylaws, and other organizational and administrative issues.

Write a cover letter to the administration about your idea, and set up a meeting to discuss it. If you have support from other parents in the school, let the administration know and perhaps meet as a group with the administration to find out what additional action may be required on your part.

How to Write It

Using personal stationery, letterhead, or good quality bond paper, type a business letter using block or semi-block format. Address the letter to the principal or administration. Start by introducing yourself, your idea, and why it is important for the school community. Outline your goals and objectives and how you plan to implement the program, including who will do what in the organization, what your bylaws will be, and other relevant information. In your letter, request guidance and support from school administration. Provide your contact information and end with a complementary close and your signature. Don't forget to provide any supporting documentation that you may have, including information from a parent organization, business plan or articles of organization, and any financial information. While this all seems very formal, presenting a professional image will let the administration know you are serious.

Letter for Starting an Organization

Marybeth Mitruchina
17 Pleasant View
Bellinghamton, WI 53562

April 23, 2008

Ms. Johanna Haynes, Assistant Principal
Bellinghamton Senior High School
351 Lincoln Road
Bellinghamton, WI 53562

Re: Band Booster Club

Dear Ms. Haynes,

Band is such an important part of the lives of many students and families, and we would like to start a band booster club at the school. Because there are many costs beyond what the district provides in order to have a quality band program, a booster club would work to defray these costs and reduce the fees that each family needs to pay toward their student's music education. Volunteer parental involvement and support are key when it comes to providing the support and encouragement for every student to reach their highest level of success.

The booster club would allow us to provide support for all aspects of the Bellinghamton Senior High School Band Program, including the marching band, symphonic and jazz bands, and the chamber ensembles. We already have a list of parents interested in participating in a band booster club at all levels of organization. There is also interest from within the community to provide sponsorships of the band booster club. We have drafted a set of bylaws and proposed meeting times. We have also started conversations with Mr. Johnson, band director and head of the music department, who is very interested in seeing a band booster club at the school.

We see the band booster club as an organization of adults interested in supporting the music programs at Bellinghamton Senior High School. The band boosters intend to raise money through fund-raising and assessments. The booster leadership—the primary group of parent organizers—will develop the booster budget with input regarding where the funds will be allocated. We believe that each family who has a child in any of the band programs will be considered a member of the boosters.

I hope that we can count on you and the rest of the administration to help us realize this dream. Please let me know what the next steps are in the process to officially start a BSHS Band Booster Club. Perhaps we can schedule a meeting with the other parents interested in organizing the booster club and Mr. Johnson in the coming weeks. I can be reached on my cell at 606-555-6412.

Thank you in advance for your time, and I look forward to hearing from you.

Sincerely yours,

Marybeth Mitruchina

Marybeth Mitruchina

CC: Mr. Bruce Johnson, Head of Music Department
     Mr. Andrew Murray, Principal

———————— **USEFUL WORDS AND PHRASES** ————————

We are proposing ___.

We would like to begin ___ at [school].

We envision ___.

Our goals and objectives are ___.

We hope you will be a part of ___.

We hope we can count on
the administration to ___.

We hope you will support our endeavor.

articles of organization

bylaws and constitution

We believe this organization [or club]
will benefit the students because ___.

Tips

Do

- background research before approaching the school with your idea.
- give as much information and details as possible so the administration or group leader understands your intentions and next steps.
- provide mission, goals, and objective statements in your cover letter.
- include names of parents or community members who are also involved or interested in helping.
- use the active voice.
- format the intentions in bullet points if you think it will project your ideas more clearly.
- be sincere.
- be professional. It will let the school know you are serious about what you are presenting.
- write your letter on letterhead or on good quality bond paper.
- offer a time when you can meet to discuss the organization or club with the school or administrators.

Don't

- forget to mention why your idea will benefit the students or the community.
- be forceful.

LETTERS OF INTRODUCTION FROM COACHES AND GROUP LEADERS TO PARENTS

Coaches and group leaders—such as conductors for the band, orchestra, or choral groups; youth-theater directors; Scout leaders; and youth-group leaders—should introduce themselves to parents and guardians before the start of the season or program. Parents welcome these letters and appreciate what to expect and what's expected of them before the season starts so there are no surprises down the road. It may seem like a lot of work, but it doesn't take much time at all and can be a way to pave a great relationship with the parents of the children who will be in your care several hours a week.

Be sure to thoroughly explain your policies or those of the parent organization, goals for the season or group, and the schedule for practices, games, meetings, or outings. Remind parents and guardians about registration deadlines and other things for which they are responsible. Include any helpful tips that you as an expert can provide.

How to Write It

Using personal stationery or regular letter-size paper, choose block, semi-block, or simple format. Type your letter, and use the active voice. Introduce yourself to the readers and tell them a bit about your background and expertise with the club, sport, or group. Outline your plan for the season or session as well as your goals. Include dates for when sessions begin, the schedule, and any other important information parents will need. You can include those as separate enclosures. Provide parents with your contact information, and close the letter by expressing your excitement about the program. End with a complementary close and your signature. You can make the letter more fun by including logos or other art.

Introduction to Parents from a Coach or Group Leader

Frances Best
33 Clinton Road
Arlington, MA 02474

August 20, 2008

Dear Flash! Team Members and Parents,

The fall soccer season is starting soon, and I am excited about the start of the U-12 Girls Soccer season. Most of you already know each other and me from previous years, as most of our team has stayed together. We have two new team members this year, Jacqui and Allison, who have both moved to the area recently. Welcome, Jacqui and Allison!

Practices will be on Tuesdays and Thursdays from 3:30 to 5:00 P.M. at Lambert Field. Practice starts promptly at 3:30 P.M. The first official practice will be Tuesday, September 9. Please make sure the girls arrive dressed appropriately for soccer practice with cleats, socks, and shin guards. Goalies should bring their gloves. Please don't forget sunscreen and water for your player. If anyone is available and would like to have a preseason practice to go over drills and skills, I am free on August 30 and September 6. We should be able to get the fields without competing with preseason football practice. Call Mrs. Dorton, our team manager, at 617-555-1356 so that she can secure a field. (Many thanks once again to Mrs. Dorton for volunteering to be the team manager!)

As always, here are a few reminders:

✧ No jewelry (on any part of the body) during practices or games, per ASC and MYSA rules.

✧ Per MYSA and FIFA rules, there is a zero-tolerance policy for parents addressing referees.

✧ Players should not wear cleats on the pavement because it degrades the cleats for optimal play. Wear sneakers or sport sandals on the pavement. (This will keep those expensive cleats from being damaged by concrete and pavement.)

✧ Uniforms will be distributed during practice before the first game.

✧ We will have the official game schedule by the end of the first practice. Games are scheduled to start the first Saturday in October.

I hope everyone had a wonderful and fun summer and is pumped up for another great soccer season! We will be setting up a group e-mail system and phone tree after the first practice, and a full calendar will be distributed once we know the game schedule. See you all at the first practice! If you need to contact me, my cell phone number is 781-555-9132. Go Flash!

Sincerely yours,

Coach Franny
Coach Franny

—————— USEFUL WORDS AND PHRASES ——————

Looking forward to the session [or season]!

I hope you're as excited for
this year's session as I am!

The season begins on [date].

We will meet at ___ for our
first practice [or meeting].

Welcome!

goals and plans

Don't forget that you will need
to provide your own ___.

We're looking forward to
another exciting year [or season]!

Summer's almost over,
which means ___ starts soon!

Practices will be held every ___.

Uniforms [or equipment] will be handed out on ___.

Those who need rides can contact ___.

Tips

Do

- ✉ keep the main letter short—no longer than two pages.
- ✉ use the active voice.
- ✉ show your enthusiasm.
- ✉ provide important dates.
- ✉ briefly mention important reminders, policies, or forms that need to be signed before the season or session begins.
- ✉ be as thorough as possible regarding the most important information.
- ✉ welcome the new members or participants and briefly introduce them in the letter.
- ✉ use enclosures if necessary and mention that they are included with the letter.
- ✉ provide a way you can be reached when you are not home, such as your cell phone number.

Don't

- ✉ be afraid to get creative. Use logos, pictures, or small pieces of art to add color to your letter.
- ✉ be negative. The first letter welcoming back a team or group should be positive.

LETTERS FROM PARENTS TO COACHES AND GROUP LEADERS

Unlike school-related situations, the opportunity to have face time with coaches and group leaders may be greater, since these activities tend to occur outside normal school and business hours. For minor things, you don't need to put it in writing. However, there are times when you will want to, such as when you want to thank them for a great season, have a planned absence, or the child is otherwise unable to participate in the regularly scheduled activities. Remember that while your situation is important to you or your child, the coach or group leader has several people to keep track of. They can only remember so many things—so put it in writing. A short note should suffice. Also remember that most extracurricular coaches and group leaders are volunteers, so while they may be fully engaged when it comes to that activity, they have their own families and work on their minds as well. Writing a short, informal note not only ensures that they have the information they need, it is a considerate thing to do.

How to Write It

Use personal stationery and handwrite or type your letter. Keep it simple, and use the active voice. The format can be semi-block or simple. Be sure to explain or describe the issue thoroughly. If it seems appropriate, request a meeting to discuss the contents of your letter in person. Remember to provide your contact information if necessary, and end with a complementary close and your signature.

Letter from Parents to Coaches and Group Leaders

Dear Coach,

We just wanted to remind you that Hillary will not be at next Saturday's game because we will be out of town for a family wedding. We will be back for practice the following Tuesday. Hillary will leave her gloves with Lisa in case a substitute goalie needs them.

Sincerely,

Michelle Emerson

Michelle Emerson

———— USEFUL WORDS AND PHRASES ————

I am concerned about ___.

I'm writing a quick note
to remind you that ___.

[Your child's name] will be back
to practice on [date].

I wanted to touch base with you about ___.

I am writing to thank you for such a
successful season. The children couldn't
have done it without you!

Your contribution to the team has
not gone unnoticed. Thanks again!

Tips ————————————————

Do

- ✉ keep the note short—no longer than one page.
- ✉ use the active voice.
- ✉ use personal stationery or note cards.
- ✉ include your contact information if the reader needs to call you or respond to your letter.

Don't

- ✉ forget to mention substitutions or changes that will be made if your child is absent.
- ✉ expect an answer or action to happen immediately.

CORRESPONDENCE FOR POST-SECONDARY EDUCATION

College is no longer just for the 18–21 set anymore. Many adults are going back to school to either complete a previously unfinished degree or continue post-graduate education. Regardless of when you continue your formal learning beyond high school or the type of degree sought—from Associate's degrees to post-doctoral degrees—the process of applying is the same.

Applying to Institutions of Higher Learning

The personal essay is an essential part of the admissions package. The college application essay is an opportunity to describe yourself to the admissions committee beyond what your grades and scores will tell them. It is also a chance to show that you can think critically and write clearly. A strong personal statement goes beyond giving the admissions committee information about your background and qualifications. It also gives them an idea of the applicant's personality, vision, and life and work goals. Those are often the pieces of information that convince an admissions committee that they want a particular applicant as a student and future colleague.

Be sure to adhere to the guidelines described in the admissions application. Format the essay according to the application guidelines. You need to be concise in your college essay, especially if there are word-count guidelines. It is also important to provide vivid imagery. In your writing, show who you are and be original.

Give the application essay the same care and attention you would give a final paper that you know is getting graded. Avoid repeating information elsewhere in the application package. Proofread, edit, and proofread again. Sample college essays are not provided here, as there are many excellent college preparatory resources available both online and in print.

How to Write It

The introduction gives the reader an idea of your essay's content. The body presents the evidence that supports your main idea. Use narration and incident to *show* rather than tell. The conclusion can be brief as well—a few sentences to nail down the meaning of the events and incidents you've described. Remember that your essay must prove a single point or thesis. The reader must be able to find your main idea and follow it from beginning to end. It's not about telling the committee what you've done—they can pick that up from your list of activities—instead, it's about showing them who you are.

Format your letter in block or semi-block format starting with your name, address (unless you are using letterhead), the date, and the addressee's name and address. Use good quality stationery, letterhead, or personal business stationery. Make sure your letter is printed on the computer. Conclude the letter by thanking the reader for their time, state how you can be contacted, and end with a complementary close before your signature.

Preparing Cover Letters for Academic Packages and Other Situations

In most cases, you will not need to include a cover letter with your admissions package unless there are special circumstances, such as a need to briefly explain visa status or gaps in your education or employment. If parts of your package are missing, explain when they can be expected and from whom. Provide your contact information and thank the admissions committee for their time. Other situations where cover letters may be required or useful are with on-campus or off-campus jobs or when applying for grants, fellowships, and other competitive programs.

Cover letters should be concise and no longer than two pages; one page is best. Print your cover letter on quality bond paper. Do not fold the letter. Instead, place it on top of all the other materials facing up. It should be the first thing the person reading your package will see.

Requesting Letters of Recommendation

When requesting a letter of recommendation from an instructor, employer, or colleague, do it in writing even if you have spoken to them about it beforehand. Because it is important for your recommendation to focus on your academic talents and accomplishments, your request letter will give the person a concrete reminder of these things. It will also remind them of when they taught or worked with you—especially if it has been a while since they did.

How to Write It

Make sure to give your recommendation writers at least one month before letters are due to complete and send in your recommendations. If you already have your forms, provide the people writing your recommendations with these forms and a stamped envelope addressed to the institution. Be sure to double-check the directions on the admissions application to see whether the institution wants the letters to arrive separately or with your entire package.

Helpful Sites to Prepare for College

www.acenet.edu/AM/Template.cfm?Section=CIP1

http://nces.ed.gov/collegenavigator

www.kaplan.com

www.petersons.com

http://school.familyeducation.com/college-prep/decision-making/36085.html

www.washington.edu/doit

Recommendation Request Letter

Alexis Young
874 Boylston Street
Bellinghamton, WI 53562

September 24, 2008

Mr. Samuel Priebe
Bellinghamton Senior High School
351 Lincoln Road
Bellinghamton, WI 53562

Dear Mr. Priebe,

Since Physics was one of my best classes last year and you asked me to participate in various after-school experiments for your research, I hope that I can ask you for a letter of recommendation for my college applications. I'm not sure if you know, but I am taking AP Physics this year.

I realize that you are very busy, which is why I am asking you so early in the school year. I have narrowed my list to seven schools—four schools that I really want to attend next fall, one long-shot school, and two safety schools. I have recently begun assembling the application materials. If you are able to write the recommendation, I will provide you with all of the required forms and information after I have had my official meeting with the guidance counselor.

Letter of Recommendation

Samuel Priebe
Physics Department
Bellinghamton Senior High School
351 Lincoln Road
Bellinghamton, WI 53562

November 14, 2008

Northeastern University
Application Processing Center
P.O. Box 120
Randolph, MA 02368–9998

Dear Admissions Officers,

In addition to completing the information required for teacher evaluation on the Common Application, I am including this statement about Alexis Young, a candidate for admissions at Northeastern University.

I had the pleasure of teaching Alexis in Physics I during her junior year at Bellinghamton Senior High School. In my 25 years of experience as a Physics teacher, I have rarely found a student who has the thirst for knowledge that Alexis does. Her dedication to her work, especially when challenged, is one that makes her not just a student but a scholar. Her attention to detail, passion for research, and overall sense of disciplined determination are qualities that will make her an asset to whatever program of study she sets her sights on.

Though Alexis is able to follow instructions and execute projects with complex analysis, she is not a follower. She is a leader in every sense of the word. Alexis possesses an infectious enthusiasm for whatever she is involved in. She has excelled in all of her courses, and unlike many students who take to the sciences, she is quite outspoken and vibrant. Alexis is so organized that she presented me with a letter to request a letter of recommendation for her at the start of the school year. It is that kind of maturity and responsibility, along with her academic and social achievements at Bellinghamton, that make her ready for collegiate study. She will be an asset to your university.

If you wish to speak to me directly about Ms. Young, I can be reached at 606-555-2300.

Thank you for the opportunity to recommend such a stellar student.

Very sincerely yours,

Samuel Priebe

Samuel Priebe

─────── **USEFUL WORDS AND PHRASES** ───────

I am recommending ___ because
he [or she] has the qualities to be successful
at this [company or school].

___ would be an asset to your
institution because ___.

As ___'s teacher for a year,
I have seen firsthand her [or his]
strong work ethic and perseverance.

I had the joy to work with ___ while ___.

___'s leadership in the classroom has
impressed us all at [school].

dedication

___ is a true leader because ___.

___ is an outstanding example
of academic excellence.

enthusiasm

passion

___ has achieved ___.

I have been nothing short
of impressed by ___.

Tips

Do

- ✉ follow the directions of the letter of recommendation or teacher evaluation form provided.
- ✉ find out if it's required of you to sign the back of the envelope across the seal.
- ✉ use school or company letterhead.
- ✉ be honest and sincere—speak from your heart using professional language.
- ✉ use the active voice.
- ✉ be sure to only speak about the candidate's relevant best qualities.
- ✉ discuss the candidate only in ways that relate to your professional or educational experience with him or her.
- ✉ offer a way to be contacted for further discussion.
- ✉ set the candidate apart by offering specific reasons why you are recommending him or her.

Don't

- ✉ mention anything that would put the candidate in a negative light.
- ✉ write more than two pages.
- ✉ exaggerate or be hyperbolic in your speech.

CHAPTER
7

Letter Writing for Children, Tweens, and Teens

LETTER WRITING IS A GOOD habit to start early. It is also a great activity for parents to do with their children to start or reinforce academic and social skills. Letter writing helps improve penmanship, literacy, and communication skills. It also fosters creativity and nurtures an interest in the world. It has the potential to boost children's self-esteem by having a person or group of people to correspond with regularly. Kids do not usually get mail except for birthdays and holidays, but letter writing can supply them the added bonus of receiving mail. And when it comes to mail, send and you shall receive.

This chapter is divided into age-appropriate categories and covers writing to family, peers, friends, and pen pals and includes how to draft thank-you notes and letters while away from parents.

STARTING YOUNG—LETTER WRITING FOR YOUNG CHILDREN (UNDER FIVE YEARS OLD AND PRESCHOOLERS)

It probably seems absurd that your preschooler can write letters. In a way it is, especially if they don't know how to write yet. But as author and family counselor Dorothy Law Nolte put it, "Children learn what they live." If you have children, you've probably noticed that they seem to want to copy everything you do or say. That means that if you write letters and notes, they'll want to get in on the action, too.

Letters from small children don't need to be complex. In fact, they don't need to be letters at all. A simple drawing and the act of folding it up, putting it in an envelope, addressing, stamping, and mailing it to Grandma is enough. The trip to the post office to mail their letter can be a fun activity for you to do together, too. As they get older and learn how to write—even if it's only their name—they can sign their letters or drawings. As they developmentally progress, slowly add other writing activities to the process. Have them speak while you write what they say or have them write short thank-you notes for gifts they've received for their birthday or other holidays. If you start them young, they will be letter writers for life.

Some of the letters small children could write include thank-you notes and general social correspondence. As discussed in chapter two, thank-you notes should not be written in the voice of the child if the child cannot speak or write yet. Instead, these notes should be written on behalf of the child by the parent and in the parent's voice. Once a child is old enough and understands the concept of writing, encourage him or her to write thank-you notes. If the note is after a birthday party, feel free to use thank-you-note stationery that matches the invitations or theme of the party. For occasions such as Christmas, Hanukkah, or other gift-giving holidays, use blank thank-you cards. Even better, use this as an opportunity to begin your child's stationery wardrobe—especially if they're taking a serious interest in writing notes and letters. A child's stationery wardrobe can include thank-you notes, notepaper or note cards, and matching envelopes. You might want to consider notepaper with lines until they have better penmanship.

How to Write It

Getting your child to write a thank-you note or other simple letter may require some prompting on your part. Find a quiet time to sit down with them and write or make it part of another activity such as art or reading. Don't expect your young child to be able to focus on more than a few notes or letters at one time—they don't have the attention span yet, so limit the letter writing to about 15–30 minutes at a time. Don't force the letter writing on them either. It will only lead to resistance on their part. Wait for a mutually good moment such as when you're also writing a letter or note.

Ask your child leading questions, not questions that get a simple "yes" or "no" answer. Some good questions to ask are:

- ☞ What do you want to write about to Grandma today?
- ☞ What do you like about the gift from Aunt Susan?
- ☞ Let's write to cousin Julie about going to the fair.

It's a good idea to get your child interested in sharing something about themselves and their world with another person. If the child cannot write yet, have them draw instead. When the letter writing begins, explain what you're doing and why in age-appropriate terms. Explain each part of the letter's anatomy. When filling out the return address say, "This is where we live." Write the date and say, "This is where we write today's date." Next, explain how you start a letter with "Dear" and the person's name, and that the rest of the letter is what you want to tell that person. Have them sign the letter at the end even if it's just a scribble. You can print their name below their "signature." Follow the same process with addressing the envelope and stamping it. When filling out the envelope say, "This is where Aunt Susan lives."

You could even turn a trip to the post office or mailbox into a fun field trip where they get to mail their letter. When writing letters and short notes, don't forget to have the child ask the recipient, "How are you?" and invite the person to write back. Instruct them to close with a term of endearment or a kind word before signing their name. Very young children can also decorate their letters with stickers and drawings to personalize them and make them even more special, especially if they cannot write well yet.

Topics to Write About for Young Children

- A new experience
- Family vacations
- Just to say "hi"
- A new pet
- The birth of a sibling
- Thank-you notes for presents and gifts
- Friends and classmates

General Note from a Young Child

Dear Grandma,

How are you? Today we went to the zoo and saw polar bears. Have you ever seen a polar bear? They were really big, but they were taking naps. But the penguins were awake and some were swimming. Then we had lunch. I love you. Please write me back soon.

Love,
Eli

Thank-You Note from a Young Child

Dear Morgan,

Thanks for coming to my party. I am glad that you came over for it. I really like the train set that you got me for my birthday. It is lots of fun to play with.

Love,

Frankie

LETTER WRITING FOR CHILDREN AGES SIX TO TEN

When children get older and are able to better grasp the concept of writing and receiving letters, encourage them to write letters to people who are meaningful to them. They can be short and simple notes just to say "hi." As with very young children, older children may still need prompting and suggestions for topics to write about such as a trip to the museum or ice skating for the first time. Encourage them to share an accomplishment or something they're excited or proud of and to use writing as a way to stay in touch with cousins or distant family members and friends. Other things they could write about include activities they have done, trips they've taken, new experiences, school, and extracurricular activities.

Another good activity to start with this age group is a pen-pal relationship with someone in a different state or country. Many companies and organizations maintain databases of kids who want pen pals.

- ↪ Student Letter Exchange *www.pen-pal.com*
- ↪ Sincerely Yours Pen Pal Exchange *www.sincerelyyourspenpals. com/home.html*
- ↪ Students of the World *www.studentsoftheworld.info*

These are just three Web sites that cater to the exchange of snail mail. Some letter-exchange companies are more geared toward teachers, but that should not keep parents from checking them out if it's something that might interest their child. As with any online site visited by children, parents and guardians should research the companies and supervise the child's activities for their safety.

Having an overseas pen pal can help kids learn about geography, other cultures, and customs as well as encourage them to form friendships with children from afar who share the same interests. Other good pen-pal candidates might be the children of their parents' colleagues and alumni friends. They may not be from another state or country, but it will foster relationships with children outside their school or group of friends.

How to Write It

Teaching the give and take of letter writing is perfect for children at this age. Encourage them to show interest in the recipient by asking questions beyond "How are you?" Let them sound out words on their own and spell words the way they think they're spelled. Offer guidance but don't write the letters for them. Aim to keep the letter short, but don't stifle their creativity. If the letter turns out longer than two pages, that's okay. Young kids tend to write big, so more than two pages is fine.

Similar to preschoolers, help set up the letter and explain each part but not in exactly the same way. When filling out the return address, ask them if they know their address and then show them where to write it. Ask if they know the date, show them where to place it on the letter, and have them write the date themselves. Go over how you start a letter with "Dear" and the person's name, and that the rest of the letter is what you want to tell that person.

You might want to have them write a draft first on a separate sheet of paper instead of on their stationery. When writing letters and short notes, have them ask the recipient questions they'll need to respond to such as questions about school, a recent family vacation, or a new pet. They should also invite the person to write back. Have them follow the same process of setting up the address fields for the envelope, then take a field trip to the mailbox or post office and show them how to stamp and mail their letter. It might be fun for them to give them money to buy their own stamp. The responsibility of asking to buy a stamp from the person at the counter, giving them money, and putting the stamp on the envelope may seem small, but it could be new and interesting in their eyes.

Topics to Write About for Children Ages Six to Ten

- ∞ A new experience
- ∞ Vacations or summer camp
- ∞ Just to say "hi"
- ∞ Thank-you notes
- ∞ New activities such as sports, scouts, and music lessons
- ∞ What they're learning in school
- ∞ Movies, books, and popular music
- ∞ Family or cultural traditions—especially if they're writing to a pen pal. Encourage them to ask their international pen pal about any traditions they celebrate that your child may be curious about.

Letter-Writing Tip for Kids: Make It Fun!

Encourage young children to decorate their letters with stickers, drawings, photos, or clippings from old magazines and catalogs. It's an easy and inexpensive way for them to make a collage or piece of personalized art to accompany a letter or note.

Letter for Children Ages Five to Ten

Dear Sophie,

Thank you for your letter. How are you? I am so glad you wrote to me. I was so excited when the mail came and it was from France. I am saving the stamps because they are so cool. Your envelope was really neat. I don't think they have that kind here. It was like a puzzle, and you write on the inside and fold it up when you are done. I have to ask my mom if they make those envelopes here and if we can get some. I'm sending you a picture of me holding your letter. I had my dad take it after we got the mail today.

You wrote that you play soccer. So do I! What position do you play? I play goalie. I just started this year, and I really like it. I love it when the other team thinks they're going to score and I make a good save.

What's the weather like in France right now? It is getting cold here, but the leaves are really pretty. They're changing from green to different shades of red, yellow, and brown because it's fall. Do they have fall in France?

What classes are you taking in school? I'm taking Math, Social Studies, Science, English, Music, Gym, and Art. I'm taking soccer, too, but that's for after school and on weekends. Hey, will you teach me some French?

I hope that you write me back soon. I am so glad that you're my pen pal!

Sincerely,

Matthew

—— USEFUL WORDS AND PHRASES ——

I'm so glad we're pen pals!

How are you?

I love you.

I miss you!

hugs and kisses

XOXO

I saw ___ when we were
on summer vacation.

We went to ___ for my
birthday last week.

Have you ever seen the movie ___?

Please write back.

Thank you for the present.

I can't wait to hear from you.

What are you doing in school?

Do you have any fun
plans for the summer?

Tips

Do

- ✉ keep a stationery wardrobe for your child.
- ✉ turn a trip to the post office into a special outing to mail his or her letter.
- ✉ integrate letter writing with another similar activity or add it to your list of quiet activities to do together.
- ✉ encourage them to share their experiences and what's happening in their lives.
- ✉ ask leading questions to prompt them for things to write about.

Don't

- ✉ hover over them while they're writing. Give them space to relax and enjoy the process.
- ✉ force them to write a letter. Make sure it is something that they want to do.
- ✉ have the letter-writing activity last longer than your child's usual attention span. More than 30 minutes will probably cause them to lose interest and want to do something else.
- ✉ ask questions that will only get a "yes" or "no" answer when you want to encourage writing.

LETTER WRITING FOR 'TWEENS AND TEENS AGES 11 TO 17

Letter writing can be used to keep in contact with others even when kids are older, despite the popularity of e-mail, instant messaging, text messaging, and social-networking sites. While the electronic age has given us the convenience of instant communication, it has a downside—especially for kids. Use of the Internet encourages writing shorthand, and kids usually don't have the tools to know when to turn off their Internet shorthand and write properly. Continuing to engage them in letter writing can help them learn grammar and sentence structure and maintain proper written communication skills.

Just as you would for young children, encourage 'tweens and teens to stay in touch with cousins and distant family friends by writing letters. At the next family reunion, make sure to get everyone's home address and then encourage your teen to write to the cousins and other relatives they had fun with that day. Giving kids their own stationery and address book so they can stay in touch may add additional incentive to write letters.

How to Write It

If they haven't already been writing letters from when they were younger, show your child how to format a simple, informal letter with the letter-writing basics. Be nearby to provide guidance or answer questions but give them enough space to feel comfortable, write what they want, and express themselves.

At this stage, letters can be handwritten or typed on the computer. Depending on their age and understanding of voice and tone, encourage them to write in the active voice. Now is also a good time to teach them when to use formal versus informal language and the different levels of respect for the recipient. In other words, explain the differences between how they would write to their friends and how they would write to Aunt Margaret or their senator. Make sure the letter is proofread before it is mailed.

At this stage, parental supervision and guidance is still necessary to a certain degree, and parents can decide how to balance that supervision and guidance with their child's sense of privacy and autonomy.

Topics to Write About for 'Tweens and Teens

↝ New experiences

↝ Vacations and summer camp

↝ Thank-you notes

↝ Activities such as sports, scouts, music lessons, and other hobbies

↝ What they're learning or have learned in school

↝ Movies, books, and popular music

↝ Their favorite celebrity

↝ Family or cultural traditions

↝ Dealing with parents and siblings

↝ Current events in the news

Letter-Writing Tip for Parents: Make It Educational!

You can use letters to teach your child many things, and that can mean more than just the importance of writing. Take this opportunity to teach them about money and other home economics such as the cost of stamps and how to mail a letter.

Letter Between Camp Friends

Dear Emily,

How are you? I was so excited when I got your letter! That's awesome that you made the volleyball team. Way to go! I can't believe what your brother said, though. He just wishes he were as cool as you and made the traveling team the first time he tried out. Ha!

I really miss everyone from camp already. I can't believe it's only been a few weeks since we got back. Have you heard from anyone else yet? When do you start school? We don't go back until the week after Labor Day. I'm actually excited to start because I think I'm going to try out for Drama Club this year. Auditions aren't until the end of September, though, so I have a while to prep. I have to come up with a song to sing since they're doing a musical. But I have no idea which musical yet. With my luck, it probably won't be *The Pajama Game*. I can sing that in my sleep! Of course there's still that part about having to tell my parents that I'm trying out. I will probably get the "Don't overextend yourself" lecture. Can you see me rolling my eyes?

I almost forgot. Thank you so much for the picture! I put it on my bulletin board. I'll send you one as soon as my mom downloads them from her camera.

I have to keep this short because we're supposed to be going back-to-school shopping this afternoon. Miss you so much! Write me back! I'd love to hear what's going on with you.

Lots of love,

Mia

Parental Awareness = Kid Safety

When encouraging your children to write letters, be aware of who they're writing to and what they're writing about. Older kids may feel like you're invading their privacy, but your awareness may protect them from potential predators. Be sure that they know beforehand what is and is not appropriate—and who is and who is not appropriate to write to.

————— USEFUL WORDS AND PHRASES —————

How have you been?

I miss you so much!

I was so excited to hear from you.

hugs and kisses

I'd love for you to write me back.

How has school been going?

Have you seen
[TV show or movie] yet?

That was so thoughtful of you!

I can't wait to send you the photos
from our summer vacation.

I'm so excited to start
[camp, club, or sport] this summer.

Tell me all about your vacation!

Congratulations on making
the [sport team, school play]!

I can't wait to come visit
you over winter break.

Tips

Do

- ✉ give your child his or her own stationery and stamps.
- ✉ give them space to write their letters and enjoy the letter-writing experience.
- ✉ encourage letter writing but don't force it.
- ✉ make sure they have enough stationery and stamps to write to you and their friends when they go to overnight camp or boarding school.
- ✉ encourage them to be themselves and express their thoughts freely.
- ✉ go over the rules for appropriate things to discuss, just as you would for using the Internet for social communication.

Don't

- ✉ hover over them when they write.
- ✉ make letter writing seem like a chore or obligation.

CHAPTER
8
Electronic Correspondence: idk what ur saying!

EVEN WITH THE PRESENCE OF postal and interoffice mail, many of us use e-mail as our main way to communicate with friends, family, and coworkers. Because we have grown so accustomed to firing off the quick e-mail whenever we want to make contact, we forget about picking up the telephone or grabbing a pen and a piece of paper to draft a quick note or memo. The popularity of the Internet highlights the decline of letter writing in modern society. Because we have come to rely so much on electronic communication today, we are more apt to quickly type something and hit send—often without spell-checking and proofreading. We have forgotten that the same rules that apply to traditional correspondence also apply to electronic communication.

This chapter covers the issues that pertain to the world of electronic writing. This includes e-mail, blogs, forums, and instant messaging as well as chat room and forum "netiquette"—an abbreviation for Internet etiquette. It's important to maintain the same standards with our electronic communication as with our written communication. We also need to know when and when not to use text messaging and chat-room shorthand, abbreviations, and acronyms. We'll also discuss online newsletters and Web articles since there has been a recent surge in their popularity.

E-MAIL

The format of electronic mail (e-mail) takes on the traditional written-memo format. Some portions of an e-mail are automatic, others you can configure so they are automatically included, such as your signature. However, you should follow the same general conventions when composing an e-mail that you would when writing on paper.

The Anatomy of an E-mail

All e-mail, regardless of which service provider you use, includes the fields below. They also automatically stamp an e-mail with its date and time, so you don't need to configure those fields.

- ☞ To:
- ☞ From:
- ☞ Subject:
- ☞ Body:

Spam: A Lunchmeat or a Pain?

Always fill in the "Subject:" field to avoid your e-mail message from being mistaken for spam. What is spam? Aside from being a lunchmeat that comes in square tins, spam is the use of mailing lists to send an e-mail message to a large amount of people. Spam e-mails are unsolicited ways to promote something, and oftentimes these e-mails are scams. E-mail is considered spam when the recipient does not grant permission to receive the message.

The Automatic Fields

The "To:" field is where you place the e-mail address of the recipient. The "From:" field is where your e-mail address goes and is usually automatically filled in when you compose or reply to an e-mail. The "Subject:" field is what the e-mail is about. It's wise to always fill in this field. In this Internet age and with the frequent occurence of spam and online advertisements, more and more people mistake a blank subject line for junk mail. If you want your e-mail to be read, it's best to avoid sending messages with a blank subject field. Keep the text in the subject field short and to the point. It's a good idea to avoid generic subject lines, such as "hello," "hi," and other similar phrases, as these can also suggest the message is spam. Unfortunately, not all spam messages get caught by spam filters and many still end up in your in-box. To avoid having your message treated as spam by either the e-mail program or the recipient, be more specific when titling your subject. Try something like "Hello, from [your name] or "A note from [your name]." Including your name in the subject line can be crucial when sending an e-mail to someone you don't regularly correspond with. A personal e-mail address alone doesn't always tell the recipient who wrote the e-mail.

The Body

Follow the conventions of standard letter writing in the body of an e-mail. For personal e-mail, start with "Dear" and the recipient's name. If you do not know the person well or if this e-mail is for business, use their title and surname. Similar to the other types of writing you do, use the active voice. However, it's okay to use the passive voice in personal e-mails because they are usually less formal and are between family and friends.

The Signature Line

Most e-mail providers allow you to set a standard signature that is automatically included at the end of every message you send. Your signature should be simple. At the very least, it should contain your name. Your signature will probably vary depending on whether the e-mail is personal or for business. When sending a personal e-mail, using only your first name is acceptable. You could also include personal information, such as your telephone numbers, URL of your personal Web site, or even a favorite quote. When sending business e-mail, regardless of whether the e-mail address you're using is your official work e-mail address or your personal e-mail address, you should be professional. Your business signature should include your first and last name, title, company name, business telephone numbers, and the URL of the company Web site. You can also include your personal cell phone number if you need to be reached for business matters while out of the office. You do not need to include any other information in your signature unless it directly relates to your job.

Some people use virtual business cards, called vCards, as their business signature. This is perfectly acceptable. When designing your signature, don't go overboard with fonts and color schemes. While some fonts appear more like a handwritten signature, others are hard to read or the font may not be supported by the recipient's e-mail service. The vCard should be simple, clear, and contain minimal flair.

Example of a vCard

Joanna Smith

Big Corporation, Inc.

12 N. State St., Suite 2

Chicago, IL 60602

Joanna.Smith@bigcorp.com

Work: 312-555-1252

Cell: 312-555-1444

Fax: 312-555-1253

How to Write It

Write in short, clear sentences and keep the e-mail as brief and to the point as possible. If you are including attachments, inform the recipient that there are attachments and, if necessary, a brief explanation of what they contain. End the note with a complementary close and your name. When composing your e-mail, use standard language instead of slipping into Internet shorthand, especially in business e-mails. "'Net speak" is too informal and not everyone who uses e-mail is familiar with the shorthand reserved for Internet forums, instant messages, and chat rooms. To be a cyber-savvy e-mailer, you need to be able to decipher when to use casual or formal language.

Some Basic Internet Terms You Should Know

ISP—Internet service provider

IP—Internet protocol is a numeric address that is given to servers and users connected to the Internet. For servers, it is the domain name (*www.yourwebsite.com*). For users, it is assigned by your ISP whenever you go online.

HTTP—hyper text transfer protocol is the prefix for most Web page addresses.

URL—uniform resource locator describes the location and access method of a resource on the Internet. In essence, it is the Web address. It also identifies a specific machine and a file or directory on that machine.

Other E-mail Features

Carbon Copy: The carbon copy (CC) and blind carbon copy (BCC) fields are where you place the e-mail addresses of anyone you wish to receive the e-mail in addition to the actual recipient. Use the "CC" field when you want the direct recipient to be aware of who else is receiving the message. Use the "BCC" field when you *don't* want the recipient to know who else is receiving the message. The "BCC" field can also be used when you're sending the same e-mail to several people, such as a newsletter to family and friends, and you want to protect each recipient's privacy, since all addresses placed in the "To" and "CC" fields will appear in every recipient's e-mail.

Priority: Some e-mail providers let you set the level of priority for an e-mail as low, standard, or high. Others allow you to receive a return receipt, which will notify you when a recipient has received and opened your e-mail.

The priority feature should be used sparingly. In other words, do not set all of your e-mails as "high priority" unless it is extremely important that the recipient read or respond to your e-mail as soon as possible. Also remember that some service providers do not recognize the return-receipt feature, so even if you have set your e-mail to send you a return receipt, you may not get one.

Don't Hit "Send" Yet

Before you hit "send," reread your e-mail and proofread it using your e-mail program's spell-check feature. If the e-mail is business related or contains important information, it's a good idea to print it out to proofread it before sending. Spell-check will not catch every typo and error. Remember that if you typed "hat" and meant to type "hit," spell-check will not catch the error, since both are real words. That may not be a huge blunder when sending e-mail to friends and family, but if you were sending a business e-mail about how well last night's fundraiser was, and you wrote, "the fundraiser was a big hat," you won't come off well.

Another reason to pause before hitting "send" is if you are sending an angry, private, or intimate e-mail. You can usually save an e-mail as a draft to send out later, sleep on it for a day or two, and reopen it to make any necessary edits before sending.

Personal E-mail, Group E-mail, and Privacy

E-mail, like any other form of written communication, assumes a certain level of privacy between the correspondents. However, its privacy is not as infallible as one might think. Written letters can be burned, shredded, or flushed down the toilet. E-mail cannot. E-mail can be traced, computer keystrokes can be recorded, and communications records are maintained by your provider.

Privacy threats are also reasons to pause before hitting "send," especially if you are using your work e-mail account at your employer's expense or are sending personal, sensitive, or intimate information. Avoid using your work e-mail for personal business. In fact, it is a violation of company policy for many businesses. This includes using work computers to check personal e-mail accounts. Not all companies enforce this, but it is a good rule to live by as a professional.

If you send a carbon copy of an e-mail or for group e-mails, you can assume that privacy is gone now that more than two people are privy to the exchanged information. If the e-mail is of a sensitive nature, consider who should receive it and only send it to that person. You can send group e-mail by inserting all the recipients' e-mail addresses in the "To" field, "CC" field, or "BCC" field. Using the "BCC" method to send group e-mail is beneficial when you do not want to share e-mail addresses with everyone else on the list. The "BCC" field is also helpful because many spam filters are set to catch bulk and group e-mails with many e-mail addresses in the "To" field. This might ensure that your legitimate group e-mail gets through. When replying to a group message, make sure you hit "reply" instead of "reply to all" unless you know every single person on the list and your response is one that every person needs to read.

Parental Guidance Suggested

Internet safety is important for all ages, especially for children. Parents need to be aware of what their children are doing on the Internet and the Web sites they're visiting. Beyond setting parental controls on your computer, it is necessary to be actively involved in your child's Internet activities. Be proactive—warn them about sharing personal information, including their last name and where they live, go to school, or teams and organizations they may belong to. Trust your instincts. If something doesn't seem right, it probably isn't. As a parent or guardian, you are the first line of defense for protecting your children.

Tips

Do

- ✉ follow the same conventions for e-mails that you would for letter writing on paper.
- ✉ keep the text in the subject field short and to the point and avoid generic messages that may be mistaken as spam or junk mail.
- ✉ write in the active voice and use short, clear sentences when possible.
- ✉ include your signature and contact information, especially in business e-mail.

Don't

- ✉ hit "send" before using spell-checker, proofreading, and checking for content appropriateness.
- ✉ send personal e-mail to business e-mail addresses.
- ✉ use e-mail addresses of people you don't know personally that you received from a group e-mail. Just because you and someone on a group e-mail list both know the sender, it does not mean they know you or want to hear from you.
- ✉ send the same message more than once. If you do so accidentally, e-mail the group or person and apologize once. Double-check any automatic features you may have set on your e-mail account to avoid repeating the same issue.
- ✉ send an e-mail with a blank subject line.
- ✉ send Internet chain letters, urban legends, jokes, and other just-for-fun e-mails to someone's business e-mail address.
- ✉ use emoticons, Internet abbreviations, or "'net speak" in a business e-mail.

ELECTRONIC SOCIALIZING— FORUMS, BULLETIN BOARDS, ONLINE MESSAGING, AND CHAT ROOMS

Internet forums, bulletin boards, and message boards have become daily activities for people of all ages. Text messages, instant messages, and online chat rooms have accelerated our ability to communicate with one another. While electronic writing is not exactly writing a letter, it is a form of correspondence. When it comes to connecting with others on forums and message boards, the rules for writing are relaxed. However, you should consider the nature or atmosphere of the message board or online forum. Most online communities are designed to bring together diverse people with common interests. These groups and forums provide a conversational atmosphere where you can interact with one another in real time. Some forums are strictly professional, others social, and some are a combination of both—like a virtual watercooler or break room. Remember that even though you use an alias as your username, you are still publicly presenting yourself on Web forums and message boards. As anonymous as you may think you are, moderators and board administrators have access to your ISP address, which can be used to identify you.

Unless your employer has relaxed rules about Internet use, avoid using online forums while at work unless it is work related. For example, it might be perfectly acceptable for a restaurant consultant to be on a foodie message board at work, but being on the message board of her favorite band while at work may not be a good idea.

Forums are meant to be fun—even the professional ones. It's acceptable to use "emoticons" (the computer equivalent to expressing an emotion, such as a smile, a wink, or laughter) and other types of flair, but they should be used wisely. Even on purely social forums, avoid overusing flair. They take up a lot of physical computer space and can make the boards slow to load. Make sure you use a legible font that is not too small or too large. Justify your text to flush left rather than centered or flush right. This will make your posts easy to read and less stressful on the eye.

Some Common Forum Abbreviations

The following is a list of generic, universal terms you may find at just about any online forum or message board. Some abbreviations may have other meanings at specific boards, and their uses will depend on the context.

BB—bulletin board

BC or B/C—because

BF—best friend or boyfriend

BIL—brother-in-law

BTW—by the way

DC—dear/darling child

DD—dear/darling daughter

DH—dear/darling husband

DS—dear/darling son

DW—dear/darling wife

EOM—end of message

FI—fiancé/fiancée

FIL—father-in-law

FWIW—for what it's worth

HTH—hope that helps

IDK—I don't know

IL/ILs—in-law/in-laws

IM—instant message

IMHO—in my humble opinion

IMO—in my opinion

IRL—in real life

ISP—Internet service provider

JK—just kidding

K—okay

KWIM?—know what I mean?

LMK—let me know

LOL—laughing out loud

MIL—mother-in-law

MOH—maid/maiden/matron of honor

NFT—no further text

NMS—not my style

NP—no problem

OMG—oh my gosh/goodness/God

OOT—out of town

OT—off topic

OTOH—on the other hand

PM—private message

ROTFL—rolling on the floor laughing

SAHD—stay-at-home dad

SAHM—stay-at-home mom

SIL—sister-in-law

TIA—thanks in advance

TMI—too much information

TX/THX—thanks

TY—thank you

WAHD—work-at-home dad

WAHM—work-at-home mom

WB—welcome back

WOHM—work-outside-home mom

WWYD—what would you do?

YW—you're welcome

Social Media Sites—Be Careful What You Post

With the number of people using social media sites increasing daily, many recruiters and businesses will do an Internet search of potential job candidates and check to see what information is available about them on the Web. This means that anyone searching for a job should be savvy about what they place on their personal Web site, blog, and social media profiles. If you're applying for college or for a job, remember that the photos you posted from a party on your social networking profile may come back to hurt you.

How to Write It

When posting on forums, message boards, and bulletin boards, use short, clear, full sentences with the exception of the accepted abbreviations of that forum. Each forum may have its own unique language, although certain terms are the same across many forums and message-board communities. Use appropriate cases and proper punctuation. Don't write in all lowercase or all uppercase. Writing in all lowercase is too difficult for other viewers to read. With the exception of some messaging abbreviations, writing in all uppercase is the Internet equivalent of yelling and should be used sparingly.

Though all forums have their own set of abbreviations, don't overuse abbreviations or text and instant-messaging shorthand beyond the accepted language of the forum. Most people find it annoying even if they are messaging savvy. With respect to any forum post, whether you're starting a thread or responding to one, consider the subject matter and atmosphere of the forum and stay on topic for the board. If you're on a professional networking forum, avoid slipping into jargon and colloquialisms that don't relate to your field. Don't use profanity. Many forum administrators set filters to block certain profane words or insert asterisks in place of a few of the letters. But even with this measure, common decency should prevail—overusing profanity says more about you than about the message you are trying to impart.

Private messages (PMs) are messages you can send to an individual via a message board or online forum. The same rules apply for PMs as they do for the public boards. Do not use PMs as a vehicle to harass or spam other members of the forum. The basic rule of thumb is to conduct yourself with the same dignity on an anonymous board as you would in real life. The point is not to stifle any sense of personality, style, or creativity, but to help you maintain your image. In the anonymous world of bulletin boards and member forums, that's the only thing most people have to know and understand you by.

The Digital Millennium Copyright Act (DMCA)

In 1998, the U.S. Congress passed the DMCA, and President Bill Clinton signed it into law on October 28 of the same year. In short, it provides copyright protection for the writers of electronic media, including bloggers, thus protecting them from content scrapers and sploggers.

BLOGGING

Blogs, short for Web logs, have become public journals and range in style and genre from professional to fun and personal and from humorous to strictly business and informational. It seems that everyone has a blog today, whether it's journalists, politicians, business professionals, your aunt, or your younger brother. Blogs can be public, where anyone on the Internet can read them, or private, where they are password protected. Readers of almost any blog can post comments with varying degrees of blog-owner moderation for accepting or rejecting comments. Some blogs are designed for comments and function as another medium for publishing articles. For example, most reputable newspapers have blog-columnists whose primary job as journalists is to blog about current events or other niche topics such as parenting, the environment, or high-tech media. Some bloggers are professionals and get paid for the posts they write. Many use their blogs as an additional way to keep in touch with a preexisting audience or to generate a new one. Others use their blogs for fun or as a way to share their ideas, opinions, and experiences.

The Basic Anatomy of a Blog

∞ Blog Title—the name of the blog

∞ Headline—the title of a blog post

∞ Body—the main text of a blog post

Fictional Blog Example

Jean's Pet Frenzy—A Pet Enthusiast's Blog

What's in Your Dog's Dish?

Today there was yet another news story about contaminated pet food. You would think that with all of the controls in place by the FDA, other agencies, and the pet companies themselves that the food we feed our "best friends" would be safe. How many dogs, cats, and other pets will have to die before something is done to protect these poor, innocent, voiceless creatures? I, for one, am not going to wait for others to make changes when I can make changes myself. It makes me wonder how safe high-end and organic pet foods are, too. People make their own baby food, so why not make our own pet food?

Other Blog Features

Categories: groupings set by the blogger that one or several blog posts may fall into. They allow readers to search for similar and related posts in a given category. For example, Jean's blog may have the categories Pet Food and News.

Scrapers and Spammers and Sploggers, Oh My!

Blogs are not immune to spam or copyright infringement. Any original idea in print, regardless of the type of media, is protected by copyright laws. Posts made by bloggers on private or personal blogs are the intellectual property of the blogger regardless of the blog host or provider. Posts made on corporate blogs are the property of the owner—unless the writer and company agreed on other terms in advance. When making posts, bloggers should make sure that they properly cite any sources they used and be aware of content scrapers, spammers, and sploggers.

Content scrapers are people or automated blogs that scour the Internet for articles and blog posts, copy your posts verbatim, and place them on another Web site or blog. Usually these scrapers will point back to your blog, but the content scraping is done without your permission. It's not appropriate because it isn't done in the same vein as quoting or citing statements you have made in the context of a new article or set of ideas. While it is not entirely illegal, it can be perceived as copyright infringement, especially because content scrapers lead back to advertising-related sites or completely unrelated blogs.

Spammers are people who use the comments field to send you and your blog readers spam. Even though many blog hosts have automatic spam catchers, some still get through. You should not click on those links, but mark them as spam and then delete them. They often lead to completely unrelated sites or a possible virus.

Splogger is short for spam blogger. A splogger is a Web site designed to look like a blog but actually hosts spam.

Tags: similar to categories, tags are set by the blogger and are more specific words or phrases relating to a specific post. For example, Jean's post about dog food may have the tags Dog Food, FDA, Homemade Dog Food, and Organic Pet Food.

Blogrolls: this is a running list of other blogs or Web sites that the blog owner likes or thinks their readers will find interesting. Some bloggers categorize their blogrolls. Jean's blogroll categories might be other pet-enthusiast blogs, pet-advocacy Web sites, or Web sites that sell some of her favorite pet products.

Widgets: these are additional things that a blogger can include on their blog, such as images, syndicated feeds, or tags for blog search engines.

Archive: this is a list by month and year of blog posts that her readers can access. Some archives include the number of posts for the given month listed. Jean's archive might look like this:

> August 2008 (4)
>
> July 2008 (16)
>
> June 2008 (22)
>
> May 2008 (14)
>
> April 2008 (9)

How to Write It

When writing a blog, almost anything goes. However, you want the voice and tone of your writing to reflect the genre and purpose of your blog, whether for business or pleasure, personal or public use. Regardless of the genre and purpose, write in clear sentences using correct grammar and spelling. Most blog programs have a spell-checker, so use it before publishing your blog posts.

Responding and Commenting

Bloggers love to receive comments to their posts even if they are set to moderate comments. Setting this feature allows a blog owner an additional measure to prevent spam and otherwise unwanted, insensitive, or inappropriate commentary. Overall, the same rules that apply to posting on Internet forums and message boards apply to conducting yourself when you post comments on someone's blog.

Anatomy of a Web Address (URL)

There are many parts to a Web address. Below is an explanation of what these components mean. Our example Web address is **http://www.yourwebsite.com/index.html**.

http://—this tells the server the type of conversion. In this case, it's hypertext transfer protocol (the most common).

www—World Wide Web

yourwebsite—this is the server being contacted when someone visits the site.

.com—this tells you the type of domain. Other common types of domains are .gov, which would be a government Web site, or .org, a not-for-profit organization.

/index—this is the file on the server being accessed.

.html—this tells you the type of file being accessed.

———— USEFUL WORDS AND PHRASES ————

blogroll

⤚

Insert text here to post a comment.

⤚

blogger

⤚

tags

Tips

Do

- ✉ conduct yourself with the same level of decorum you would in person, despite assumed anonymity.
- ✉ check with forum administrators and moderators when in doubt.
- ✉ avoid profanity—overusing profanity says more about you than about your message.
- ✉ avoid writing long-winded posts. Keep posts short and direct.
- ✉ think before you post something very personal, especially if you are unsure of the atmosphere of the forum.
- ✉ write in standard sentence structure and use the active voice with short, clear sentences whenever possible.
- ✉ avoid writing in all capital letters. Writing in all uppercase is considered yelling on the Internet.
- ✉ use emoticons and flair, such as pictures, sparingly. They can take up a lot of Internet space when overused.

Don't

- ✉ visit forums that are not work-related at work.
- ✉ use Internet forums to harass or bully other posters. Treat others as you want to be treated.

E-NEWSLETTERS AND E-ZINES

E-newsletters and e-zines have become a popular business and social tool. They allow people to keep up with news and information by sending regularly-scheduled e-mails. For the business person, it can be a great way to keep existing and potential clients informed about your products and services or they can become an added value to already-existing services. To that extent, they can be a great marketing tool. For family and friends, they can be a fun way to keep those who are geographically distant updated with your news and notes. Businesses should be careful when using the term 'zine because it denotes an amateur publication. However, even if the electronic publication is an amateur production, it does not have to look like one.

As with any correspondence, consider your audience. If you are writing an e-newsletter or e-zine for your company, maintain a professional appearance and use the language and tone appropriate for your business or industry. If you are writing for social reasons, the rules are more relaxed and you're allowed to be more casual in your language and tone. Overall, the language can be formal or informal in e-newsletters and e-zines. Write in the active voice with short, clear sentences. Be sure to print out and proofread the document before electronically sending it to your group list. Make sure you provide a way for readers or subscribers to opt out by including an unsubscribe link or instructions for

What's a Platform?

Platform is a term usually used by professional nonfiction writers to describe their built-in audience. The term platform is gaining wider use as more and more people are writing articles using self-publishing, vanity-publishing, and ghostwriters. A celebrity who has left Hollywood to start her own business and writes a book about starting her own business has a bigger platform than the small business owner who started his business from the ground up and writes a similar how-to book. You may think this is unfair. True, but the celebrity has the built-in audience of fans who are familiar with their work and will be itching to buy their book. On the contrary, Mr. or Mrs. Business Owner only has the audience of current and former clients, family, and friends. This is why many people have turned to Web articles to increase their audience and, in turn, increase their platform.

how to stop receiving your e-newsletter or e-zine. Also include instructions for the recipients to add the address from which the e-zine or e-newsletter is sent to their address book to ensure delivery to their in-boxes and not their spam or junk folder.

For most e-newsletters and e-zines, it is best to send them as part of the body of your e-mail. Remember that many people are concerned about receiving viruses from attachments, even from e-mail addresses that are trusted. To maintain your recipients' privacy, place all the e-mail addresses in the "BCC" field.

Some e-Zine and e-Newsletter Statistics

According to www.zinester.com, there are 19.4 million e-zine subscribers and nearly 4,400 e-zines distributed each month. These statistics are based on the registered users of Zinester, thus the actual number of e-zine subscribers and producers may be even higher.

So Everyone's a Writer Now: What You Need to Know About Web Site Content and Internet Articles

The Web and its rules change rapidly. What was acceptable for a Web site and Internet optimization a year ago may not be acceptable tomorrow. One recent Internet trend is to include content-related or keyword articles on Web sites for Search Engine Optimization (SEO), or the process of increasing the number of visitors to a Web page by ranking high in the results of a search engine. Internet articles are also used by many people who are self-proclaimed experts in their field but who are not necessarily professional writers. They do this to improve their search-engine ranking or for self-promotion.

There are even article banks where amateur and professional writers submit their articles on a variety of topics. Some pay the writers, others do not. Because of such services, the quality, content, and length of the articles vary. When writing such articles—especially if you aren't a professional writer—be sure to use the standard conventions for syntax, sentence structure, grammar, and punctuation. Write in the active voice whenever possible. Always write in clear sentences and proofread your articles before submitting or publishing them to the Web. In fact, it is a good idea to have another person read the article for content and clarity. You could hire a professional proofreader or editor or have a close friend or associate provide feedback.

The Anatomy of an Article

The parts of an article are:

- ☞ Headline
- ☞ Byline
- ☞ Hook
- ☞ Body
- ☞ Conclusion

An article consists of a headline, byline, hook or opening sentence, body, and conclusion. Optional article elements are sidebars, resources or references, statistics, and images. The headline is the title of the article. The byline is the name of the author. If the article is ghostwritten (written by someone else but in the author's voice), the name of the person who paid for the ghostwriting goes in the byline. It is assumed that ghostwriters stay anonymous unless other arrangements have been made between the ghostwriter and the author. The hook is the opening phrase or phrases that will draw the reader in and compel them to keep reading. Throughout the body of the article, use the active voice to keep the reader engaged. Where necessary, cite sources that you may have used for support. In the conclusion, do not simply restate what you wrote, but move toward the logical point of your article. Some articles include a brief biographical sketch of the author and a way to contact him or her, such as a Web site.

───────── USEFUL WORDS AND PHRASES ─────────

opt in

opt out

To subscribe to our e-newsletter, where
you will receive weekly updates and
have access to our special features,
please provide your e-mail address.

Click here if you no longer wish
to receive our e-newsletter.

e-zine

unsubscribe

subscribe

To ensure delivery to your inbox
(and not your spam or junk folders),
please add [newsletter e-mail address]
to your address book.

e-newsletter

Click here to learn more
about our privacy policy.

Tips

Do

- ✉ write clearly and use the active voice.
- ✉ pay close attention to grammar, spelling, syntax, and sentence structure.
- ✉ always proofread and have a second pair of eyes proofread it as well.
- ✉ cite the sources you used in the article.
- ✉ include a short biography of the author.
- ✉ provide your readers with a method to unsubscribe from your e-zine or e-newsletter in every issue.

Don't

- ✉ send e-newsletters or e-zines to people who have not subscribed to your list or have not indicated interest in receiving news from you.
- ✉ send your e-zine or e-newsletter as an attachment. Instead, send it as the text in the body of the e-mail.

CHAPTER
9

Special Circumstances

NOT ALL LETTERS ARE EQUAL. Not all recipients are created equal. Some recipients deserve a certain degree of respect, and there are correct ways to address them and ways to formulate your writing.

This chapter will discuss how to handle special situations where you need to address dignitaries and other members of society. It will cover writing to members of the clergy; writing to politicians such as members of Congress, senators, and the president; writing to leaders of other nations—for example, how you address the prime minister of England is different than how you would address the prime minister of Japan; and writing to celebrities.

We have so many options for receiving news from around the world. Many on-air options run all around the clock, and the Internet is always on. This means that public figures we only heard about years ago when something important happened now enter our lives when even the most miniscule detail occurs. While it's fantastic to have access to news about everything and nearly everyone, it also means that the lines of familiarity can be blurred. Add to that our growing sense of being casual in lieu of being formal, and you have a recipe for potential faux pas when contacting dignitaries, heads of state, the clergy, or even celebrities.

YOUR IMMEDIATE WORLD— CONTACTING LOCAL POLITICIANS, OTHER ELECTED OFFICIALS, AND CIVIL SERVANTS

There are proper channels of communication and chains of command when it comes to contacting your local and national political leaders. Some prefer a more casual approach, while others prefer a deferential one. When in doubt, it is better to assume the latter and approach writing your letter with a sense of respect for the leader and the leader's position regardless of your personal opinions about them or their policies. In the end, a letter that shows your respect for their position is one that is more likely to get a response.

Before writing, make sure you do some background research. Most politicians have Web sites that tell you the best way to contact them, whether by e-mail or standard post. If you are unsure of how to contact the politician, you can usually find contact information at the Web site for the larger body on which they serve. For example, if you want to contact your state representative, you can probably find his or her information at your state's Web site, *www.*[your state].*gov,* under Representatives and the district for which they serve. If you know their personal address, do not use it for business issues. Since their business is politics, their political address or the address they supply for their contact information is the one you should use.

Regardless of whether you choose to send a letter electronically or through the mail, use the same level of etiquette. Note that if you send a letter by standard mail, chances are someone else may be responsible for opening the mail and passing on letters to the leader. Keep this in mind when drafting your letter. Weigh your words and tone carefully. Most representatives want to hear from their constituents, so writing to them is not a waste of time. Remember, however, that the men and women who serve us are very busy, and it may take some time to receive a direct response.

Contact Information for Local Leadership and Civil Servants

Below are Web sites where you can find contact information for local and national politicians. Each state's Web site will also have listings for the local legislative communities by county and city.

- ☞ President or the president's Cabinet: *www.whitehouse.gov*

- ☞ U.S. Congress: *www.house.gov*

- ☞ U.S. Senate: *www.senate.gov*

- ☞ National Governors Association: *www.nga.org*

- ☞ U.S. Conference of Mayors: *www.usmayors.org*

- ☞ Legislative Offices by State: *www.globalcomputing.com/states.html*

- ☞ All U.S. Legislative Offices and Government Information: *http://www.usa.gov*

How to Properly Address Civil Servants

Using either the block or semi-block format for business letters, include your full name and address, followed by the date, the recipient's title, name, and address. If it's an elected official, the name line on the address could read "The Honorable" followed by their first and last names. For example, the address for a council person could read,

The Honorable John Johnson, Chairman

Your City Council

City Hall

1234 Main Street

City, State ZIP

It is better to err on the side of caution and use the more formal address when writing to your leaders instead of adopting a casual tone. While it may feel you know them because you see, hear, and read about them often, they are the leaders of thousands or sometimes millions of constituents. While they want to hear from you, they don't know you personally. To use President George W. Bush as an example, you would not open a letter to him with "Dear George." Addressing the president like that would be inappropriate. Also, remember that certain civil servants do not lose their titles once they have left office. When writing formerly seated officials such as former vice presidents, presidents, and secretaries of state, you should continue to use that title. If you were writing former President Clinton, you would address him as "Dear President Clinton."

Give and Take

When contacting your local political figures, be sure to include your contact information so that the representative or someone from their office can contact you on their behalf. Do not assume that they kept the external envelope that had your return address on it.

Also, do not assume that they will have the ability to access public records for your information if your address or telephone number is listed. If you expect a response, be sure that you provide them with a way to contact you.

Constituent Etiquette: Tone, Voice, Style, and Presentation

Even if you disagree with a leader's policies or personal life, avoid writing angry, venomous letters or making personal attacks. If you feel the need to do that, go ahead and write it. Just don't send it. As with any form of hate mail, it is best to write the letter, let it sit for at least a day, and then revisit the letter. Remove anything rude or inappropriate. Use the active voice. Depending on who you are writing, you can use a formal or informal tone; the former is preferred if you do not know the person well or if they hold a high office such as a member of the president's Cabinet, a high-ranking military official, or an ambassador or a dignitary. Use clear, short sentences. Your letter should be typed and printed on standard, letter-size paper. Use personal stationery with full-size sheets if you have it, but regular blank paper will suffice. Do not use your company letterhead unless you are writing on behalf of the company. Keep your letter brief—no longer than two pages, although one page is better. If necessary, include your district, precinct, or parish so that the reader knows exactly which constituent base you are from. If you are writing with a question or concern, include your contact information so that the recipient or one of their staffers can contact you. End the letter with a complementary close followed by your name and signature. Do not write in all capital letters, avoid slang, and be sure to proofread. You may want to have another person read your letter to ensure the best presentation possible.

How to Write a Positive Letter

People in leadership positions usually hear from people around election time or when a constituent disagrees with something. If you are pleased with your leaders, don't hesitate to write them to tell them so. Using the proper format, tone, and style just discussed, write a simple and direct letter. Be specific about what policies or legislation you are praising them for when necessary.

Civics 101: The Legislative Process

Are you confused about how the government works? Below are excellent resources for understanding the legislative process.

☞ *www.senate.gov*

☞ *www.house.gov*

☞ *http://thomas.loc.gov/home/lawsmade.toc.html*

☞ *www.centeroncongress.org*

☞ *http://www.lib.umich.edu/govdocs/legchart.html*

Positive Letter to a Politician

Ruth Dickson
12345 Logan Lane
Santa Barbara, CA 93101

April 15, 2009

The Honorable Michael Wellington
California State Assembly
State Capitol
Room 2148
Sacramento, CA 94249

Dear Representative Wellington,

Thank you for being a champion for the woodlands and wetlands in our community. We appreciate all the work you have been doing to get the new bill (S.R. 0001) passed to prevent an overabundance of corporate development in the wooded areas some think is "vacant" land.

We live adjacent to ten acres of woodlands, and it is one of the few green spaces left. As both a homeowner and a lifelong resident of my town, we have watched building after building go up and tree after tree torn down, never to be replaced. Many of the woodland animals are displaced from their homes, to the point where they have become a public nuisance because the only places they have to go are to residents' backyards.

We thank you for continuing to press forward with this bill to maintain and preserve these areas.

Very sincerely yours,

Ruth Dickson

Ruth Dickson
35th District

How to Write a Negative Letter

There are two types of negative letters—those that get read and responded to and those that do not. The letters that get responded to (or at the very least, taken seriously) are those that are well formatted, clear, concise, and rational. The better you present yourself, the more likely your letter will be taken seriously. Do not attack the person or their policies. Simply stating that you disagree with Policy X or Legislation Y is enough, along with a brief explanation of why you disagree. You can offer suggestions for what you think should or could be done, but bear in mind that the legislative process is defined by a certain set of rules. While your suggestions may be taken into consideration, any implementation is at the mercy of the legislative process and budgetary restrictions.

Negative Letter to a Politician

Joanna Allcot
12345 Sweetwater Lane
Taylor, MI 48180

August 6, 2008

The Honorable George P. Smith, Chairman
Taylor City Council
1200 Main Street
Taylor, MI 48180

Re: Protective Berms and Fencing at Sweetwater Village Condominiums and Subdivision

Dear Chairman Smith:

I am writing on behalf of the other residents of the Sweetwater Village Condos and Subdivision. Six months ago, I approached the Council during open business at the February 6 Council Meeting regarding the residents' concern about the berms and fencing that the developer of Sweetwater Village did not install as promised and still has yet to install.

As residents, we are all concerned about the risk caused by not having the fencing or berms in place. We are also troubled by the fact that many of the early buyers in the subdivision made purchases based on the land plans that were shown to us by the developer or our real estate agents.

We were promised by the Council that the matter would be looked at, but we have yet to see a resolution or hear of any progress being made.

Additionally, in the six months that have passed, we have conducted some of our own research, the results of which have led to an increased concern and need to see a resolution as soon as possible.

Our independent research has revealed that by not having the fences or berms placed, the developer is in violation of City ordinance No. 235-C regarding the construction and placement of berms or fencing along residential buildings, schools, and other similar structures that are less than 100 yards from a road with a speed limit in excess of 35 mph. Garrision Avenue's speed limit has been raised to 40 mph since our initial presentation to the Council.

Our concerns have remained unanswered by the developer, and as such, the Sweetwater Condo Association Board has turned to the city for assistance in this matter. Please do not let us down—the safety of our children depends on your involvement and pursuit of our concerns. We look forward to your response.

Sincerely yours,

Joanna Allcot

Joanna Allcot
President, Sweetwater Village Condo Association Board

If you are intent on seeing a significant change, there are proper channels to do so. That usually involves creating and filing a petition, getting a requisite number of signatures of registered voters, and officially submitting it to the clerk's office of that level of government.

How to Write a Thank-You Note to a Politician

Occasionally there is cause to write a thank-you note to a leader. Leaders are bombarded with requests to make various types of public appearances, from grand openings and ribbon cuttings to local Little League season openers and presentations at corporate events. Of course, they cannot be everywhere at once. But many try to at least make an appearance, especially when it comes to key events held by their constituents. No, this doesn't mean you should invite your senator to your wedding, unless of course, you know your senator personally. But you can invite your senator to the grand opening of the new corporate headquarters in your town.

When dignitaries are able to attend an event, be sure to thank them in person as well as on paper. A simple note written in semi-block format and with proper formatting for a business letter will suffice. If the individual or staff member on their behalf appeared at an event for your business or organization, use that letterhead for your thank-you note. Keep the note simple and use the active voice. Thank them for their time and for what they did such as giving a speech, holding the keynote address, making a presentation, or simply showing up. Express your gratitude for their presence and for taking time out of their busy schedule. Don't forget to include the date and function that they attended. End the thank-you note with a complimentary close followed by your name and signature. You may include a business card with the thank-you note as well.

Thank-You Note to a Politician

Dear Congressman Frederickson:

We were very glad that you were able to attend the groundbreaking on May 15 for the new Conservatory and Botanical Gardens that are being built by the Epstein Garden Club in honor of its founder, Ms. Mildred G. Epstein. We realize that you are pressed for time, but we are grateful for the wonderful sentiment you delivered at the event. Had she been alive, Ms. Epstein certainly would have been pleased and honored.

Many thanks for your continued support.

Very sincerely yours,

Jane B. Merryweather

Jane B. Merryweather
President, Epstein Garden Club

Finding the Appropriate Title for Your Politician

Below is a list of titles for various political leaders and how you may address them. You should begin your letter with "Dear" and the appropriate title plus a comma.

Executive Branch

- President: "Dear Mr./Madam President," or "Dear President [Surname],"

- Vice President: "Dear Mr./Madam Vice President," or "Dear Vice President [Surname],"

- Secretary of State: "Dear Mr./Madam Secretary," or "Dear Secretary [Surname],"

- All members of the Cabinet: "Dear Mr./Madam Secretary," or "Dear Secretary [Surname],"

- Attorney General: "Dear Mr./Madam Attorney General," or "Dear Attorney General [Surname],"

Judicial Branch

- Chief Justice: "Dear Mr./Madam Chief Justice [Surname],"

- Justice: "Dear Mr./Madam Justice [Surname],"

Legislative Branch

- Speaker of the House: "Dear Mr./Madam Speaker of the House," or "Dear Speaker [Surname],"

- U.S. and State Senate: "Dear Senator [Surname],"

- U.S. House of Representatives: "Dear Congressperson/ Congressman/Congresswoman [Surname]," or "Dear Representative [Surname],"

- State House of Representatives: "Dear Mr./Madam [Surname]," or "Dear Representative [Surname],"

State and Local Municipal Government

- ∞ Governor: "Dear Mr./Madam Governor," or "Dear Governor [Surname],"

- ∞ Mayor: "Dear Mr./Madam Mayor," or "Dear Mayor [Surname],"

- ∞ Chairperson of a local council: "Dear Mr./Madam Chairperson," or "Dear Mr. Chairman/Madam Chairwoman,"

- ∞ Councilman or Councilwoman: "Dear Councilman/Councilwoman [Surname,]"

GREAT EXPECTATIONS—WHAT TO EXPECT AFTER YOU SEND YOUR LETTER AND HOW TO ASK A QUESTION THAT WILL GET A REPLY

Even though our representatives work for us (their constituents), do not expect them to be able to respond to every letter you write. Like you, they are pressed for time, have multiple meetings and engagements, sit on various committees, and handle several issues at once. Also, do not assume that sending an e-mail will warrant a response more quickly than sending a letter through the regular mail. If you want or expect a response, include your contact information and the best way and time to reach you. You can also include the phrase, "I look forward to hearing from you or your staff," which is a clear indication that you hope to receive a reply. If you do not expect or want a response, only include your address and your district information.

Give your leader ample time to reply. If you have a question about a certain policy or piece of legislation, they may need extra time to research the issue in order to give you the best response possible. Be candid and direct in your letter but not forceful. If your letter warrants a follow-up response, don't be afraid to make a follow-up call to the individual's office a few weeks after you send your letter.

―――――― USEFUL WORDS AND PHRASES ――――――

I am writing to thank you for ___.

⤚⤙

We are interested in
learning more about
[bill name and number].

⤚⤙

I am disappointed in the recently
passed [bill name and number]
because ___.

⤚⤙

I am writing to tell you that your
constituents are concerned about ___.

⤚⤙

Thank you for attending ___.

⤚⤙

The Honorable ___

⤚⤙

Respectfully yours,

⤚⤙

Thank you for your continued support.

⤚⤙

I look forward to hearing
from you or your staff.

⤚⤙

We are presenting this
petition in hopes of ___.

⤚⤙

Dear Mr. [or Madam] ___,

⤚⤙

Your constituents are grateful for ___.

Tips

Do

- ⊠ use standard letter-size paper or personal letterhead.
- ⊠ use business block or semi-block format.
- ⊠ write in the active voice and use clear, short sentences.
- ⊠ include your contact information if you would like a response.
- ⊠ be direct but not forceful.

Don't

- ⊠ write in all capital letters.
- ⊠ use slang and other colloquialisms.
- ⊠ make personal attacks or threats.
- ⊠ expect an immediate response, especially if your letter is regarding a certain piece of legislation.

YOUR IMMEDIATE WORLD— CONTACTING YOUR CLERGY

Most people do not have a regular need to contact their clergy by mail, since most members of an organized religion see their clergy members about once a week. However, sometimes it's necessary for special circumstances such as arranging a ceremony or an event involving your religious institution. Even if you have a personal relationship with your clergy leader, you should defer to the respect of their religious office and title when writing to them.

Some forms of address for members of the clergy include:

- ↬ Bishop
- ↬ Brother (for monks and certain fraternal orders within the church)
- ↬ Cardinal
- ↬ Deacon

- Father
- Imam
- Monsignor
- Mother
- Pastor
- Rabbi or Rebbe
- Rebbizen—the Rabbi's wife, who may occasionally give counsel
- Reverend—in writing should be preceded by "The"
- Sister—when referring to nuns
- Your Eminence—reserved for the highest orders of the church hierarchy
- Your Excellency—also reserved for the highest orders of the church hierarchy

Tone

Your tone when writing a member of the clergy will depend on the nature of the letter and your comfort level with one another. If the letter is regarding an official event, such as confirming arrangements for marriage class, an official ceremony, or the annual youth group's spring event, you should use the formal tone. If the letter is personal, then the casual tone may be used. Writing to local religious leaders will most likely warrant a casual tone because you are more familiar with them and see them more frequently. When writing to clergy you don't know personally or who are of a higher office than your local clergy, use formal language and tone.

Your letter can be formatted in block, semi-block, or informal style. The style should match the nature of the letter and the person's religious office. As always, include your name and address, the date, and the clergy person's proper title, name, and address. Start the letter with "Dear" or "Esteemed." Keep the letter brief and no longer than two pages. Use the active voice with short, clear sentences. Conclude the letter with a complementary close, your name, and your signature.

Letter to Clergy

Mr. Charles Goren
404 Briarwood Road
Belleville, MI 48111
March 3, 2008

Bishop James Beckwith
Bishop of Detroit
4500 St. Mark's Avenue
Belleville, MI 48111

Your Excellency,

On behalf of the parish of St. Agatha's in Belleville, I want to thank you for your continued support of our Youth-in-Crisis program. This encouraging program provides guidance and assistance to teens in our community. The program does this without question for those who may be on the wrong path, regardless of religious affiliation. Your speech to the parish and group leadership emphasizing our moral responsibility as stewards of the community was inspiring to all who attended.

Thank you again for your unending support and inspiration.

Very sincerely yours,

Charles Goren

Charles Goren
St. Agatha Parish, Youth Group Leader
Youth-in-Crisis Program

cc: Father Marcus McIntyre, St. Agatha Parish

I FEEL LIKE I KNOW YOU—
CONTACTING CELEBRITIES

No matter your age, you may occasionally feel the need to write a celebrity. We constantly see them on television and in magazines and newspapers. Sometimes we love them and sometimes we hate them as we watch their professional and personal lives being scrutinized in the media. Chances are if you write to a celebrity, someone from their staff will respond. If they have an official fan club or Web site, use that information to contact them. Do not try to find their home address to send them mail. Type and print your letter and be sure to include your name and address, followed by the date and their fan-mail address. Keep your letter brief—no longer than one page.

If you want to write a celebrity, there are positive ways to do it. Do not declare undying love for them or present personal attacks. Don't include gifts or spray your letter with perfume or cologne. Make the letter simple and to the point—either sending praise for their latest accomplishment such as an Academy Award or success from their latest hit song. However, don't approach writing a letter to a celebrity with the expectation that you will get anything in return. You may get a signed photo, poster, or quick note from their staff thanking you for your support, but chances are you will receive nothing. Writing celebrities is probably the only case where your letter-writing efforts will not be reciprocated. However, many celebrities and personalities have blogs or other social media sites for consistent fan contact, so going the electronic route may be your best bet if you feel the need to write to them.

THE "REAL" NEWSMAKERS—
CONTACTING THE MEDIA

Americans are an opinionated group. In reality, we are not more opinionated than our counterparts around the world; we just tend to share our opinions more frequently and candidly. We tend to do this verbally or in writing and to people we don't even know. The real newsmakers—that is, the people responsible for bringing the news to us—are part of our daily lives. Our comfort level with them and with sharing our opinions leads many to contact their local newspaper editors and television and radio anchors. Either way, we read about their work or see and hear them deliver the news on a daily basis. The same is true for other media personalities such as disc jockeys and talk-radio hosts.

How to Write Reporters and Letters-to-the-Editor

The news moves quickly. Deadlines and turnaround times for reporters and editors are so quick they would make most heads spin. Timing is everything. If you intend to write a reporter, columnist, or a letter-to-the-editor, it is important to do so as close to the publication's print or air date as possible. Whether in print or online, all newspapers and magazines have contact information on the masthead at the very least. If the publication is in print, the masthead is usually within the first few pages of the periodical, somewhere after the table of contents and a series of advertisements. If the publication has a Web version, the information should be listed on the "Contact Us" page. Some publishers include guidelines for submitting letters-to-the-editor or opinion letters. Always follow these guidelines when submitting letters-to-the-editor or when contacting reporters, and include any information that the publication requests. Not following those requests could be the difference between getting your letter published and getting it thrown in the trash.

Whether sent via e-mail or by regular post, your letter should conform to the basic conventions for business format. It's a good idea to draft the letter in a computer program such as Word and then cut and paste it into the body of an e-mail once you're satisfied. Include your name, address, the date, and the editor's, reporter's, or columnist's name and department. Also include the name of the periodical and its address. Open the letter with "Dear" followed by the journalist's surname. Do not write "Dear Editor," or "Dear Reporter," and do not address the person by their first name unless you know them personally. When writing an editorial or a response to a specific article, be sure to reference the date, issue, and title of the article in your letter.

How to Write a Reporter, News Anchor, or Other Journalists

One can never emphasize it enough—the world of journalism moves quickly. Deadlines are sensitive and a topic may be interesting and important, but if you don't give the journalist enough time, your letter doesn't fit that issue's theme, or there is more important breaking news to report, your letter may be bumped to the "later" pile. Unless you are simply writing to provide a news tip or consumer alert, find out the lead time—how far ahead of the print date you need to contact the outlet in order for a story to be included in the next issue. When writing to anchor people, radio personalities, and talk-show hosts, consider your audience—there's a big difference between writing a political analyst and writing a controversial disc jockey.

GREAT EXPECTATIONS—WHAT TO EXPECT AFTER YOU HAVE SENT YOUR LETTER AND HOW TO WRITE A LETTER TO GET A REPLY

To maximize the chances of getting a letter-to-the-editor printed or receiving a response from a reporter, your letter should flow well and remain on topic. Write in the active voice with clear sentences. Keep the letter brief and no longer than one page. Longer letters are less likely to be printed. Also remember that if your letter-to-the-editor is printed, it is subject to editing and cutting for length or content. Avoid slang and colloquialisms and never use profanity, even if it is mild profanity. You should know the audience and genre of the publication to which you are writing—letters-to-the-editor for a financial magazine would be a stark contrast to letters-to-the-editor for a women's magazine. Be sure to include your contact information. Don't worry, if it's printed, that information will be edited and only your name, city, and state will appear.

If you want your letter-to-the-editor to be printed in the "Opinions" section, your letter about your lazy children to be printed in the advice column, or your news about the local Girl Scout Troop's community service project to be picked up by a local reporter, you need to give the journalist a reason to separate your letter from the countless others they receive. Some media outlets receive hundreds of letters a day. Therefore, your letter must be well written and needs to have a strong and compelling opening. After all, you are writing to journalists—the very people whose business is words—so you want to be grammatically correct. Make sure your letter doesn't have spelling errors or typos and that you get to the point of your story or letter quickly and succinctly. Don't be discouraged, however, if the letter does not get printed or if the news story is not included. There are many stories vying for journalists' attention, including local, national, and international news stories with weight that may trump your story or letter. However, your letter will have a higher chance of getting a response or of being printed if you follow these tips and suggestions.

Letter-to-the-Editor

Dear Mr. Hearst,

Kudos for printing the "Local Teen Gives Back" article in the Wednesday, December 16, edition of the paper. It was a beautiful story and a wonderful alternative to the negative news we usually hear and read regarding our teens. Jason should serve as an example to his peers, and his parents have obviously done something right. I applaud them, as well.

Sincerely yours,

D. Moore

D. Moore
Allentown

——— USEFUL WORDS AND PHRASES ———

Thank you for your
support and inspiration.

I am writing to congratulate you
on your recent success with ___.

Job well done on your
recent article on ___!

Thank you for shedding light on
___ in your article about ___.

I look forward to hearing from
you or a member of your staff.

I am writing to respond to [article name]
from your most recent issue.

I was disappointed to read that ___.

I continue to appreciate
[newspaper or magazine]'s
cutting-edge stories and original ideas.

I have been an avid reader of
[newspaper or magazine] for years,
and your recent story on ___ reminded me why.

Bravo on uncovering the
recent corruption by ___.

Tips

Do

- ✉ write in the active voice.
- ✉ keep your letters brief and no longer than one page.
- ✉ be sure to write the correct person, editor, reporter, or columnist.
- ✉ remember your audience and the style and tone of the publication.
- ✉ always follow the media outlet's instructions for letters-to-the-editor.
- ✉ use the correct form of address and formality.

Don't

- ✉ include slang or profanity.
- ✉ automatically expect a response when contacting a celebrity.
- ✉ forget to include the specific article and issue date when writing a letter-to-the-editor.

CHAPTER
10
International Relations

As a global society, we communicate with people from far away on a daily basis. We often forget that we're communicating with non-U.S. citizens because so many people are proficient in English and are able to communicate with us effectively in our first language. In some cases, their English may be better than ours! But some things do not translate well, such as idioms, colloquialisms, and slang. Unless someone is fully immersed in and well acquainted with a culture, it is unlikely that a nonnative speaker will understand.

On a similar note, it is wise to understand and recognize the conventions of formality and speech that are different from our own when contacting someone abroad. Special attention should be given to the nuances of international communication. We'll give you some pointers on how to read and understand different international conventions and how to apply them in your writing when necessary.

WRITING ABROAD

When conducting foreign business, it is important to be aware of the social etiquette and customs of the person you're writing. Occasions when you'll need to have direct communications with someone abroad may include:

- ↩ Travel—making or confirming arrangements for business or pleasure
- ↩ Working with companies, distributors, or service providers
- ↩ Communicating with coworkers in a global company or a business with satellite offices abroad
- ↩ Transacting business or communicating with an online company or business representative based abroad
- ↩ Working with museums, libraries, or other institutions for research, securing images, or requesting permission for images for a publication

How to Write It

Use the same format and conventions that you would use for formal business letters. To ensure understanding, it is best to opt for a more formal voice and to write in clear, simply structured sentences. Be as specific and detailed as possible to ensure that there is no confusion about terms, agreements, or arrangements. It's important to be polite and to choose your words carefully. This is because emotion can be hard to convey in the written word, and phrases that we casually use in the United States may be misconstrued or taken the wrong way by a nonnative English speaker. Keep words simple—this isn't the time to show off your vocabulary.

A Tale of Two Englishes

From an American point of view, there is no mistake that we speak English. But to non-Americans—including the British—that is debatable. The difference lies in whether you speak the Queen's English, sometimes called British or Continental English, or whether you speak American English. The languages are very similar, however certain spellings are different. For example, "color" (American English) versus "colour" (British English), or "realized" (American English) versus "realised" (British English).

There are also differences in word usage between American and British English. For example, what Americans call a "diaper," the British call a "nappy." What Americans call a "sweater," the British call a "jumper." If you frequently contact people in Britain, the

Oxford English Dictionary is useful to keep handy. There are complete versions as well as abbreviated desktop or pocket versions available. It will help demystify some of the words and phrases you're unfamiliar with as well as allow you to write without causing confusion on the other end.

Oh, Canada!

Canadian speech seems to be a hybrid of American and British English. Some Continental English conventions remain intact such as spelling and some grammatical usage. But overall, there are clearly defined rules for spelling and grammar in Canadian English that are neither British nor American. If you are writing to someone in Canada, the *Gage Canadian Dictionary* is a smart thing to have on hand. The good news is that even if you don't have this resource, your writing will still be understood if you write in clear, short sentences and use the active voice. Pay close attention to whether you are writing to someone in Quebec versus the other provinces. Quebec, having retained its French identity, is more formal than many of the other Canadian provinces. While French and English are recognized languages, opt for writing in English unless you are fluent in Canadian French.

Contacting Heads of State

On the rare occasion that you will contact a head of state in the United States or abroad, there are certain rules of protocol that must be followed. This includes etiquette regarding preferred titles and forms of address. Every country has different ways of addressing their leaders, so be sure to research the title and proper greeting of the leader you are writing before you begin. In general, when contacting a foreign leader, use their official title such as President, Doctor, His/Her Royal Highness (H.R.H.), His/Her Majesty the King/Queen, and so forth instead of Mr., Mrs., or Ms.

When communicating with members of nobility, it is proper to use either courtesy or honorary titles. Capitalize King, Queen, Prince, and Princess when the title precedes a name. In the United Kingdom, the convention is to provide full titles for the ranks of nobility below sovereigns. Dukes are referred to by their

Some Titular Positions for Heads of State in the United States and Abroad

- ☞ Admiral or Vice Admiral
- ☞ Ambassador
- ☞ Brigadier
- ☞ Captain
- ☞ Commander
- ☞ Chairman
- ☞ Chancellor or Vice Chancellor
- ☞ Chief of Cabinet
- ☞ Colonel
- ☞ Deputy
- ☞ Doctor
- ☞ Field Marshal
- ☞ General
- ☞ His/Her Royal Highness (H.R.H.) for regents
- ☞ Lieutenant
- ☞ Major
- ☞ Marshal or Vice Marshal
- ☞ Minister of Foreign Affairs, Cultural Affairs, Trade, State, etc.
- ☞ President or Vice President
- ☞ Prime Minister or Deputy Prime Minister. The Prime Minister's full title is Prime Minister, First Lord of the Treasury, and Minister for the Civil Service.
- ☞ Professor
- ☞ The Queen of England should be addressed through The Private Secretary of Her Majesty the Queen. Her title is Her Majesty, Queen Elizabeth II.
- ☞ Rear Admiral
- ☞ Reverend
- ☞ Secretary of Defense, State, etc.

first name followed by their royal location. For example, Sherman, Duke of Yorkshire, and his wife, Duchess of Yorkshire. You would not refer to the Duchess of Yorkshire as Lady Anne or Duchess Anne. The terms Lord and Lady are used for the children of the duke. Marquess, Earl, Viscount, and Baron should always be capitalized, and their proper title should be used in formal address. As with the duke's family, their children are given the titles Lord and Lady. The female counterparts to the aforementioned noble ranks are Marchioness, Countess, Viscountess, and Baroness. These titles should only be capitalized when they precede a name. For those who are not of noble blood but who have honorary titles such as knight, use the term Sir before their name. Give the full name preceded by Sir when first addressing someone, and Sir [First Name] after that.

Shall I Call You Ambassador?

According to the document "Protocol for the Modern Diplomat" from the U.S. Department of State, special note should be made on how to address ambassadors. In the past, only active ambassadors or ambassadors who retired with the personal rank of career ambassador were allowed to use the title. However, that custom has changed. Now, those who have served as ambassador after Senate confirmation may continue to use the title. They may be referred by the title of ambassador in conversation or when introduced to public audiences. However, regulations permit the use of "Ambassador, Retired" for ambassadors who have retired from service.

Although the United States does not use the term Excellency, some countries do when referring to ambassadors. Even if the host country uses the term Excellency, Americans may be addressed as Mr. or Madam Ambassador by U.S. citizens. Foreign chiefs of mission who are accredited to the United States are also referred to as ambassadors.

Lost in Translation

Imagine you need to contact someone abroad, but you're not sure of their fluency in English. Or, you think that it will be better to write in the person's native language to bypass the potential misunderstanding and then translate your letter in English with online translation software. Stop. Do not touch the translation software. It seems like a good idea at first—to have instant translations made for you at the push of a button or click of your mouse. The problem is that most translation software is grossly mechanical and misses idioms and the other unique flourishes of language. Your formerly well-crafted letter will seem ridiculous when translated by this software.

Ich bin Berliner: the Blunder that Never Was

Many sources throughout recent history have claimed that John F. Kennedy made a major blunder in his famous "Ich bin ein Berliner" speech at the Berlin Wall in Berlin, Germany, in 1963. According to the story, he said "Ich bin ein Berliner," when he should have said "Ich bin Berliner." The correct phrase means "I am a citizen of Berlin." However, his faux pas told the nation, "I am a jelly doughnut." While a "Berliner" is in fact a type of jelly doughnut made in Berlin, a 1993 article by Jürgen Eichhoff offers this analysis of Kennedy's statement: " 'Ich bin ein Berliner' is not only correct," he wrote, "but the one and only correct way of expressing in German what the President intended to say." Only a true citizen of Berlin would say, "Ich bin Berliner."

Eichoff explains that in proper German grammar, the indefinite article *ein* is required to express a metaphorical identification between subject and predicate. Otherwise, the speaker could be taken to say he is *literally* a citizen of Berlin. And thus, President Kennedy spoke correctly. Additionally, his grammar was flawless because he took the care to enlist a native speaker to translate the phrase for him.

Given all of the possible confusion, it is better to write the letter in proper English unless you can correctly translate into a foreign language yourself. If you are fluent or proficient in a foreign language but may need some assistance, rely on your trusty English-to-foreign-language dictionary and grammar books and avoid the free translation software altogether.

Tips

Do

- write in the active voice.
- use simple, standard speech.
- pay special attention to phrases and terms used in British English that are not used in American English.
- write in a formal and polite tone.
- use business format—either block or semi-block style.

Don't

- begin your letter before doing some research—make sure you're addressing the recipient correctly.
- use translation Web sites. Instead, rely on foreign-language dictionaries or write the letter in English.
- use slang or colloquialisms that do not translate to another language.

Index